VIRTUE,

SUCCESS,

PLEASURE, &

LIBERATION

Other books by Alain Daniélou

The Complete Kama Sutra
Gods of Love and Ecstasy
The Myths and Gods of India
While the Gods Play
Yoga: Mastering the Secrets of Matter and the Universe

VIRTUE,
The Four Aims of Life

SUCCESS,
in the Tradition

PLEASURE, &
of Ancient India

LIBERATION

Alain Daniélou

Inner Traditions International
Rochester, Vermont

Inner Traditions International
One Park Street
Rochester, Vermont 05767

Library of Congress Cataloging-in-Publication Data
Daniélou, Alain
    Virtue, ambition, pleasure, and liberation : the four aims of life
in the tradition of ancient India / Alain Daniélou
        p.   cm.
    Includes bibliographical references and index.
    ISBN 0-89281-218-4
    1. Life—Religious aspects—Hinduism. 2 Hindu ethics.
I. Title.
BL1215.L54D36 1992
294.5'4—dc20   92-25844
                                                        CIP

Printed and bound in the United States

10 9 8 7 6 5 4 3 2 1

Text design by Charlotte Tyler and Bonnie Atwater

Distributed to the book trade in the United States by American International Distribution Corporation (AIDC)

Distributed to the book trade in Canada by Publishers Group West (PGW), Montreal West, Quebec

CONTENTS

NOTE
FROM THE PUBLISHER

Today we hold up egalitarian democracy, equality of the sexes and races, and multiculturalism as our social and political ideals. We are constantly reminding ourselves and being reminded that this is the common good toward which society has been "evolving." However, if we view the contemporary world with a degree of objectivity, we will observe that the sexes, races, and various cultures are all faced with constant propaganda and pressure to be assimilated into a mode of human existence consistent with the goals and values contained within the perception of reality and the imagination of Western progressive commercial society.

Wherever assimilation and adaptation to these goals and values are resisted, conflict, oppression, and exploitation occur. Three-quarters of the wars being fought in the world today are conflicts in which cultural and ethnic groups are struggling against political and economic entities known as states or countries with internationally recognized and accepted borders. "The First World," comprising only 20 percent of the world's population, enjoys 66 percent of the world's income. Struggles between the interests of black and white, north and south, tribal and modern peoples have taken center stage, replacing the discredited ideological fight between east and west. The inconsistency between our "ideals" and these horrifying world realities makes it imperative for us to investigate and explore other social orders that existed prior to the advent of the prevailing Eurocentric world view. It is in this spirit of inquiry, and not as a formula, prescription, or answer to our present problems, that this book is offered.

Prior to its colonization, India was the most culturally diverse nation on earth. How is it that all its different races, cultural groups, lifestyles, religious practices, deities, and languages (more than fifty) survived for more than five thousand years to the present day? What is the nature of the social order that unquestionably produced one of the greatest and longest lasting civilizations known to man? Alain Daniélou, distinguished Orientalist, musicologist, and linguist, challenges us to enter the Hindu worldview on its own terms and journey through its life cycles from virtue to success, from pleasure to its final goal and destination . . . liberation.

Ehud C. Sperling
Publisher

INTRODUCTION

Virtue, Success, Pleasure, and Liberation is an unusual work: it is an intricately conceived, extended metaphor. It might be called a "metaphoric gestalt" that expands into an innovative and revelatory conceptual system in which human social order, spiritual unfoldment, and biological development are all set in a cohesive integrated vision, drawn from Alain Daniélou's reflections on the ancient texts and Sutras describing traditional Hindu society. The development of this metaphoric gestalt is based on the correspondences and relationships that spring from a natural fourfold division in seemingly unrelated areas of human experience:

> The four stages of biological development: childhood, youth, maturity, old age
>
> The four seasons of the year: spring, summer, autumn, winter
>
> The four areas of human accomplishment: virtue/devoutness, success/material acquisition, nobility/aesthetic and sensual refinement, knowledge and detachment/spiritual liberation

1

The four racial colors of humanity related to the four earth
pigments: black, yellow, red, white
The four castes of traditional society: the worker/artisan,
the producer/merchant, the warrior/aristocrat, the
scholar/priest/mystic
The four elements of traditional philosophy: earth, air,
fire, water
The four spatial directions: south, east, west, north

In all traditional societies throughout the world, though the
details may vary, this fourfold division can be found. Without ex-
ception it symbolically represents the foundational order required
for the creative consciousness to structure itself into a physical
reality. The traditions that maintain the philosophy of fourfold
order of physical manifestation are diverse in time and location.
They range from Australian aborigines to Native Americans to
tribal Africans to Chinese and Japanese Taoists to the peoples of
ancient India and Egypt to Sufi mystics to medieval alchemists and
to European Renaissance humanists and architects. The same fourfold pattern reappears in the content of contemporary science: the
four major fields of force, the four elements basic to organic substance, the four geological types of rock, the four major tissue
types of the body.

The method of developing an analogic or metaphoric structure based on a numerical form pattern such as duality, trinity,
or quaternion is a fundamental procedure in all esoteric philosophy. In fact, the further back one reaches in history and prehistoric cultures the more one finds that language and symbolism rely
upon number/form analogy and are increasingly metaphoric in exposition. Historically, we can view a gradual decline in the metaphoric nature of language. Shakespeare, standing at the threshold
of the major conceptual shifts that occurred in the seventeenth
century, foresaw the tragic fall of language into the rigid mold of
objectivism and logical positivism. To Shakespeare this marked a
foreboding and ominous destiny for mankind, particularly European culture.

The Sanskrit texts from which Alain Daniélou draws his re-

2

search are of this pure analogous dynamic. Metaphor and analogy function on one and the same principle: *the understanding or experiencing of one kind of thing in terms of another*. Very often, in modern language, this entails a process of thought in which a nonmaterial experience or process is understood in terms of a physical one that bears some similarity to the former. For example, the statement "He attacked every weak point in my argument" is based on the metaphoric analogy of an immaterial process (argument) understood in terms of physical combat (war). This linguistic habituation, of understanding and depicting immaterial experience from objects and examples in the physical world, we have retained, as a vestige, from the view of reality that prevailed before the Age of Reason and the scientific revolution. Before this profound shift, which definitively separated the inner and subjective from the external and objective, the world was imaged as manifestations of one indivisible reality appearing in its visible and invisible forms. The condition of the human body, likewise, was considered the visible appearance of one's mind and spirit, just as mental activity was an expression of the individual's way of sensing his physical embodiment.[1] Language, in this world view, was the field in which these inner and outer processes and images were brought into confrontation and relationship and where one could track the unlimited potential of metamorphosis, back and forth, between visible and invisible experience.

Since the reign of science and logical positivism, language has been considered to have a completely different function. The process of language is to achieve, in words, a precise descriptive "fit" with what is considered a separate, objective, external reality. With this focus we forget the hidden metaphoric origin of language. For example, we can make what we consider a purely factual statement: "She fell asleep but fortunately woke up in time to avoid an accident." This simple statement contains several unacknowledged

---

1. E. C. Whitmont, *Psyche and Substance* (Berkeley, Calif.: North Atlantic Books, 1991).

metaphors of spatial orientation: "conscious is up" (woke up) and "unconscious is down" (fell asleep).[2] These and innumerable other hidden metaphoric processes become unacknowledged beliefs and biases within our culture. Of course, the "conscious is up" and "unconscious is down" metaphors are based on bodily experiences: we normally tend to lie down or fall over in an unconscious state, and we do spend much of our conscious time in an upright posture.[3] However, this is only an external and singular perspective. From another point of view, an internal one, unconscious states such as sleep, dreams, reverie, meditation, and trance can be our most expanded and elevated moments, whereas active awake consciousness is very often our most grounded, confined, and mechanical mode.

Modern language and modern conceptualization are dependent upon unacknowledged metaphoric gestalts in which an invisible world of experience is reduced to, and understood in terms of, physical objects. We routinely convert intangible time, duration, and events into objects; thoughts and ideas become substance; states of being and emotion are transformed into material containers.[4]

The Sanskrit language, and the thought processes with which Alain Daniélou has conceived this work, never deny or disguise the metaphoric basis of language. He never forgets that the transformations in our understanding that metaphors can provoke are a "trick of hand," which only *highlight* the way in which apparently different things are similar and, at the same time, temporarily *hide* the way in which they are different. For example, when he draws an analogy between the archetypal qualities of the black race and the archetypal qualities of childhood, it is not intended as a factual assertion but rather as one element from a complete metaphoric gestalt or extended analogy: "The black race is to the white race as childhood is to old age, as spring is to winter, as wet and

---

2. G. Lakoff and M. Johnson, *Metaphors We Live By* (Chicago: University of Chicago Press, 1980).

3. Ibid.

4. Ibid.

moist are to cold and dry, as south is to north." This entire series of analogies is based on highlighting some qualitative similarities while momentarily diminishing variations, diversions, and dissimilarities.

One can consider that metaphor is to language as resonance is to sound: the metaphoric highlighting of similarities between widely divergent areas of experience creates an inner resonance, a musing on the mysterious connectedness of all things. Also characteristic of this holistic process of thought is the idea that a sense of totality is achieved only when a state is fused to its own opposite or inverse. For example, while we muse on the possibility that the black race, with its characteristic spontaneity, rhythmic sensuality, and joyousness, is the childhood of humanity, we also recall the inverse of this proposition: that childhood is also the "father" or predecessor of the adult human. The complementary play of a statement or viewpoint with its own opposite is a fundamental and valuable aspect of analogical thinking.

The ancient Hindus did not take lightly the resonant nature of analogical language for establishing meaning but used it as a guide for creating harmony in their social structures. The analogous patterns based on the phases of human maturation—childhood, youth, maturity, and old age—set the form for the initiatic passages, particularly in the lives of Hindu men. Women's lives are given biological definition and developmental patterns: puberty, menstruation, childbirth, menopause. However, the education of male psychosexual energy, with its propensities toward aggression and power, has posed a problem for all cultures throughout the ages. The focus on male development in Daniélou's exposition of Hindu society (which prior to Vedic and Islamic intervention was more matriarchal in nature) is due to the fact that a woman's roles and spiritual unfoldings are given by natural cycles, whereas male development must rely upon the wisdom of his society and cultural forms. For this reason, Hindu society is worth close scrutiny, in that contemporary society is plagued by the competitive, destructive, warring excesses of uninitiated men and by uncultivated, male-dominated religious, economic, and political systems.

India was the first, the largest, and—for millenia prior to Islamic and European colonization—the most enduring and successful multiracial, multicultural society in the world. The model of Hindu society can provide a rich, complex language of far greater depth than our conventional, simplistic, egalitarian, democratic ideals. To allow this language to reach us, in reading Daniélou's work and meeting in it many inevitable challenges to our sensibilities and beliefs, we will do well to recognize that the Hindu world view is here presented on its own terms.

Our conditioning has tricked us into believing that language is supposed to provide clear absolute statements concerning factuality or truths. With language denied the sense of metaphor, we easily forget that there is no such thing as an external objective world, separate from the perceptual and linguistic processes through which we experience and describe that world. We forget that everything in our perception exists only in relationship to another thing. No language can either encompass or describe the diversity and vastness of the external world, and no term in any language can completely describe or encompass the qualities or another term from that language. As with metaphor, all language, whether poetic or scientific, can only highlight aspects of our experiential world while obscuring others.

It is not difficult when one is operating in the analogical mode to commit blasphemy against the prevailing religion of rational positivism and against the unacknowledged biases and hidden moral codes that emerge from the objectivist view of language and reality. Because Alain Daniélou has applied this unfamiliar thought technique in dealing with issues that are presently so vital and controversial, such as race, social caste, individual rights, sexual behavior, marital practices, and spiritual attainments, his path is doubly fraught with danger. I hope that these preliminary remarks will allow the reader to enter this work in the intellectual spirit in which it was created and thereby benefit from the fresh perspectives and broad vistas it provokes.

Robert Lawlor
Flinders Island, Tasmania, 1992

Part One

1 THE HISTORICAL BACKGROUND

HISTORY AND LEGEND

The Hindu lives in eternity. He is profoundly aware of the relativity of space and time and of the illusory nature of the apparent world, and therefore attaches only secondary importance to the events of his time. He envisages history as a series of cycles, whose development leads humanity more or less to its point of departure. The Hindu historian seeks an image or reflection of these cosmic laws in terrestrial events. In everything, in every destiny, he sees the immediate presence and direct action of metaphysical forces, which may symbolically be called gods, since their real nature surpasses our understanding. History interests the Hindu only insofar as it evinces eternal law and divine manifestation. It is punctuated by the incarnations of the gods, which are called *avataras,* or "descents." It is the history of the gods, permanent beings, and their relations with the ephemeral world of the living which is the only true history and the only one that really matters. For us it is a source of learning.

There are very few ancient Hindu texts of what is called history in the Western world. The "Ancient Chronicles," or Puranas, and the "Epics," or Itihasas (a word that means "once-upon-a-time") mix mythology and history; the genealogies of kings and legends of the gods; scientific, philosophical, and moral teaching; and folk memories of prehistoric migrations. The Hebrew Bible is considered by the Hindus to be a Purana of the Mlecchas, or barbarians, and it indeed contains several elements borrowed from more ancient traditions. Many of the Purana texts known today are written in late, popular Sanskrit and are relatively recent translations and compilations of very ancient texts written in the various pre-Aryan languages of India. Furthermore, there are versions of the Puranas in several Dravidian languages, which are older than the Sanskrit versions. Important passages have been interpolated and added to the Purana texts over the centuries, and nothing remains of the original manuscripts, which may have been written in lost languages. However, these vast works contain a vast quantity of information about the remotest periods of history. The genealogies, which go back to the sixth millennium B.C.E., are probably largely authentic. The stories and descriptions of the various regions of the earth and the various civilizations living on the "seven continents" provide priceless documentation on the world's oldest civilizations.

A critical study of the Puranas has yet to be made. Most of them have been given only partial publication in Indian editions that are already obsolete, and only two or three—the more literary but not the most important—have been translated into Western languages. The publication and translation of the Puranas would be a considerable task, as there are eighteen principal and eighteen secondary Puranas, some of which are larger than the Bible: thirty-six works in all. There are numerous recensions of each, showing important variations. The twenty-two volumes of the *Skanda Purana* take up half a shelf in my library. Among the Epics, the *Mahabharata* alone fills twelve volumes.

In order to understand the history of ancient India we must reconstruct it piece by piece, starting from widely dispersed but often precise data found in works whose purpose was not to describe history as we understand it but rather to create a moral code, a philosophy, or even a mythology of history.

The first peoples to inhabit India belonged to a very ancient race, related to the aborigines of Australia and the hill tribes of Indochina as well as to the most ancient African populations. They still live in the forests and high plateaus of the interior in India, speak the *munda* languages of the paleolithic epoch, and do not practice agriculture, which they consider to be a violation of Mother Earth. Their society often takes matriarchal forms. Some of these tribes have developed an urban civilization and, being in closer contact with later invaders, have gradually lost their own tongue. Nowadays they form certain workers' castes and have maintained extremely ancient oral traditions, both religious and social, about their kingdoms, kings, and cities, in almost forgotten ages.

The first great civilization of India of which important traces have been found is that of the Indus, whose cities, abandoned since the second millennium B.C.E. and now covered with sand, give evidence of a highly refined urban civilization. It should not be thought, however, simply because of the geographical and climatic accident which preserved these particular cities, that civilization was confined at the time to that part of India, or that the Indus civilization was necessarily the most ancient. Most of the great Indian cities already existed at that time, but their wood and mud structures could not withstand centuries of monsoons. The Puranas repeatedly refer to the sixth millennium B.C.E. as an important period of scientific and artistic development. The great urban civilization of India that reached its height just before the Aryan invasions developed between the sixth and the third millennia, and it was this civilization that gave birth to Shaivite religion and philosophy.

Who were these ancient Indians? Very probably they spoke Dravidian languages, since pockets of these languages still remain in the northwest of the Indian continent, while their grammatical infrastructures (syntax, word order, grammatical forms) subsist in the popular languages of northern India, and in Hindi in particular. This suggests that these languages, with their almost entirely Aryanized vocabulary, developed among peoples who had formerly spoken Dravidian dialects. The contributions of munda or Dravidian languages to classical Sanskrit, an Aryan language, have not yet been seriously studied.

The Dravidian-speaking peoples who now live in the south of India are not autochthonous. They came to India during a very remote period, perhaps from Africa or from a lost continent located between India and Africa, as their legends tell. They are dark-skinned and have straight hair. Certain ethnic characteristics, especially discernible in their hemoglobin, appear to indicate a nonnegroid African origin, as do some cultural aspects such as the predominant rhythm of their music.

Africa knew important civilizations during the prehistoric and protohistoric periods but became severely depopulated for unknown reasons. A role may have been played by epidemics like those that decimated some of the American peoples before the arrival of the Europeans. In the very fertile areas of East and Southeast Africa, however, the present inhabitants are mostly recent arrivals. We know little of the peoples that utilized the vast workshops of prehistoric weapons and tools.

According to their own legends, the Dravidians escaped to India from a sunken continent to the south of Kanya Kumari, the cape of the Virgin, now called Cape Comorin, India's southernmost point. The date they give for this catastrophe is more than ten thousand years before our era, and a part of their most ancient poetry, belonging to the first *sangham,* or "Poets' Club," is supposed to have been written on their now submerged territory.

However likely it is that apart from the munda languages, Dravidian languages were spoken throughout India before the Aryans' arrival, the races speaking those languages today are not necessarily the same. Each successive civilization pushed its predecessor southwards, and it could well be that Southern India became merely a Dravidian colony, which alone managed to keep its ancient culture, just as the non-Aryan south became the refuge for a great part of Sanskrit culture during the period of Islamic domination.

The Aryans were a white-skinned, pastoral people, who came

down from the steppes that today form part of southern Russia and Turkestan, about 3000 B.C.E. They crossed the mountains of Afghanistan and broke in great numbers over the Punjab, the land of the five rivers converging in the Indus estuary. Gradually they conquered the whole of the Ganges plain and central India. They were nomads and had been pushed south probably by climatic conditions. They never lost their nostalgia for their northern habitat, that country called in the Puranas Uttara Kuru (North Kuru), where there flows a great river and where the sages and the ancestors live. Further north was the polar mountain, the dwelling place of the gods, where each night and each day lasts six months.

These rough and courageous Aryans discovered a marvellous civilization in India—cities of gold and silver with splendid palaces and incalculable riches, offering every pleasure. These cities were inhabited by a dark-skinned people, who worshipped the phallus and the snake, and who fought bravely against the invader. The protracted war that ensued became for the Aryans the symbol of the eternal conflict between the white gods and the black demons, the war of the *Devas* and the *Asuras*.

When the Asuras lost, they were reduced to the status of second-class citizens, thus forming the basis for the future low castes. When they defended themselves successfully, however, the wars ended in treaties that recognized the princely titles of the dark-skinned sovereigns, who thus became "honorary Aryans." To a great extent, they could then keep their states and their own culture.

The Asuras had philosophers, scholars, architects, and artists of all kinds, and their science was unequalled. As a result of this contact, the Aryans became city-dwellers and their sages came to learn from the Asura masters, thus giving rise to the philosophy of the Upanishads and to the traditional Hindu sciences and arts. Many of the Asura masters were included in the Aryan list of prophets and were venerated along with the Aryan sages who had composed the hymns of the *Rig Veda*. All subsequent religious, philosophical, ritual, and historical texts—the *Atharva Veda,* the Brahmanas, the Aranyakas, and certain parts of the Puranas,

13

Agamas, and Tantras—are the fruit of reciprocal influences by Aryans and non-Aryans at different periods throughout the long history of India.

Sanskrit became the main vehicle of culture. Virtually nothing remains of the original texts of the Indus civilization, except a few barely deciphered inscriptions. The language or languages spoken are unknown to us, although it is almost certain that they were Dravidian in type. Little effort has yet been made to explore the remnants of Dravidian literature, in particular the texts in ancient Kanada, of which whole libraries still exist in the Shaivite and Jain monasteries around Mysore. Researchers have been put off by the immensity of the preliminary work, the difficulty of access to the manuscripts for non-Hindu Shaivites or Jains, and the problems of classification and of dealing with archaic alphabets.

The Shaivite rites still practiced in the south of India are clearly pre-Aryan, in particular the burial of the dead in underground chambers together with all their familiar objects intended to serve them in the next world. By contrast, the Aryans—originally nomads—cremated their dead. The relationship of the Shaivite rites to other great pre-Aryan civilizations such as the Sumerian, Cretan, and early Egyptian is quite evident. The cults of Osiris and Dionysus are late survivals of Shaivite religion.

THE BIRTH OF A CIVILIZATION

When the Aryans first established dominion over the Punjab, they were conquerors who despised the urban luxury of the original inhabitants. The Puranas and Itihasas give lengthy descriptions of battles that are a transposition to a mythological and heroic level of the battles between the invaders and the indigenous population. As the Aryan empire was established, however, its customs were gradually relaxed by contact with the "demons," who had by now become men whose wisdom and skills could be acknowledged and whose religion and philosophy could be adopted from many points of view, thus posing new problems that are common to all great empires. How could permanent Aryan domination be assured at

14

the same time as a durable peace? It was necessary to find the means to hold sway over many races with different languages, whose level of culture ranged from the man of the forest to town dwellers accustomed to all the refinements of civilized life. Each element of the population in the Aryan empire had to have its own place and to be satisfied with it. Many diverse cultures had to be preserved in order to put to use their advantages and skills, while at the same time the Aryans themselves must not be swallowed up by repeated social and political alliances.

It is clearly impossible after so many centuries to know how the rules and laws first evolved that would create the framework within which multiracial India found stability while allowing its civilization to develop for so long in harmony. Hindu scholars have recently expressed the view that the founding of Hindu society must have been the work of a brain trust. Men of astonishing vision and wisdom drew up a plan giving a livelihood to all while avoiding racial mixing and the senseless destruction of the institutions, customs, and ways of thinking and acting that differed so widely from one people to another.

This plan may have taken many centuries to be implemented, but there is little doubt that it was conceived on a rational basis, abstractly, with an intelligence and prudence that modern peoples might well have emulated had they wanted their empires and their civilizations to last.

The organization of this corporative society, which we know (not very well) under the name of the caste system, had to ensure for every element of the population an inviolable means of subsistence and the right to keep its beliefs, its own social and civil institutions, and its gods, festivals, and customs. This system allowed the Aryan civilization to assimilate and employ all the conquered peoples, without either destroying them or being dissolved by them and without imposing any great change in their beliefs or way of life. Here is probably one of history's great lessons in the art of governing. This theory is found in many political treatises, the most ancient of which are a mere three thousand years old, all referring to even more ancient texts. Many of the former have become annexes to Vedic literature, while others form part of the Puranas and Itihasas. There are also collections of laws and political works, such as those of Manu (*Manu Smriti*) and Yajnavalkya (*Yajnavalkya Smriti*), attributed to sages of the Vedic Age. To these must be added Shukra's "Politics" (*Shukra-niti*) and numerous later treatises, such as the *Artha Shastra* by Kautilya, written by a minister to one of the Maurya emperors in the third century B.C.E.

SANSKRIT

The first and perhaps most important of the great achievements of the Aryan empire was the creation of an artificial language, both ideal and perfect, known to us as Sanskrit. The word *sanskrita,* meaning "refined," or "purified," is the antonym of prakrita, meaning "natural," or "vulgar."

Sanskrit is actually an ideal improvement of Vedic. The original sacred language of the Aryans, Vedic had developed in contact with the other languages of India and given rise to numerous Prakrits, which are the forerunners of the Aryan languages of modern India, such as Hindi, Bengali, Maitili, Punjabi, and Gujarati. Even with the Dravidian languages, ancient texts are now dated according to the increasing proportion of Sanskrit terms used.

The Sanskrit grammarians wished to construct a perfect language, which would belong to no one and thus belong to all, which would not develop but remain an ideal instrument of communication and culture for all peoples and all time. We no longer possess the first grammars of classical Sanskrit but have only fragments and quotations referring to those of Indra, Chandra, Kashakritsna, and others which preceded Panini's eight-chapter grammar (the *ashtadhyayi*), composed as a summary of all the grammars prior to the fifth century B.C.E. Panini's grammar became a model for its clarity, concision, and simplicity. Enlarged by numerous commentaries, this grammar is still used in the teaching of Sanskrit today. However, the commentaries on Panini and works by semanticists and philosophers interested in the nature of language and its connection with thought mechanisms, such as Nandikeshvara's *Kashika*

16

and Bhartrihari's *Vakyapadiya,* refer to grammars that are older and less scholarly than Panini's.

Sanskrit was a complete success and became the language of all cultured people in India and in countries under Indian influence. All scientific, philosophical, and historical works were henceforth written in Sanskrit, and important texts existing in other languages were translated and adapted into Sanskrit. For this reason, very few ancient literary, religious, or philosophical documents exist in India in other languages. The sheer volume of Sanskrit literature is immense, and it remains largely unexplored. Being interested in musical theory, I have collected more than one thousand texts on that subject, ranging from the fifth century B.C.E. to the sixteenth century C.E. Not even ten of these texts have been published up to now, and only three have ever been translated. The situation is identical for all the other disciplines—history, philosophy, astronomy, geography, medicine, and so on.

Probably we shall never know well our own history over the past five millennia until this immense reservoir of Sanskrit documents has been tapped. It is deeply to be regretted that no modern organization is interested in examining even a few of them seriously. Many texts disappear every year, since the manuscripts are highly perishable in India's extreme climate, and the teams of scholars who once used to recopy damaged manuscripts for the libraries have almost entirely disappeared.

Sanskrit is constructed like geometry and follows a rigorous logic. It is theoretically possible to explain the meaning of the words according to the combined sense of the relative letters, syllables, and roots. Sanskrit has no meanings by connotation and consequently does not age. Panini's language is in no way different from that of Hindu scholars conferring in Sanskrit today. Indeed, scholars from the various provinces of India have no other means of understanding and conversing with each other. Sanskrit has always been and remains the language of cultivated people. In classical theatre, princes, Brahmins, ministers, and officers speak in Sanskrit, while servants and often the women reply in the various Prakrits.

The Persian of the Mohammedan period and the English of today have been but poor substitutes for Sanskrit as instruments of culture and means of communication among the various peoples of India. These languages are not as closely connected with the roots and concepts of the Indian tongues and rapidly degenerate into dialects, soon becoming unintelligible from one province to another.

2 THE BASES OF SOCIAL ORDER

THE CYCLES

According to Hindu cosmological theory, matter is merely appearance, and the universe formed only of energy relations. At the root of everything, we find a relation between a centripetal force that condenses, a centrifugal force that disperses, and the balance of the two, giving rise to a circular motion that determines movement, whether of stars or of atoms. Space and time are immeasurable. Nothing of itself is either big or small, and an instant is not less than a millenium. Time and space exist only in relation to living beings, whose perceptions determine spatial dimension and whose vital rhythms measure time, thus making them entirely relative.

For man, the universe is thus measured by his vital rhythms, such as the beating of his heart, which give him his dimension. We can perceive only those aspects of the universe whose pulsations lie within certain limits of light and sound. Waves whose frequency is either extremely slow or extremely fast for us form universes of which we know nothing. By extending this concept—not to individuals, who are merely the links in the chain of a species, nor even to a single species, mankind, but to all forms of life as we perceive it—we see cycles appear. We see then that we are merely tiny parasites belonging to the solar system, and that our vital rhythms are fundamentally linked to the movement of earth and the planets. We are conditioned by the duration of day and night, the year's cycle and the cycle of the moon.

All forms of individual or collective existence are conditioned by series of cycles contained within each other. This is inevitable, moreover, because duration, one of the coordinates of existence, is only a rhythmic division in the substratum of time. The cycles of day and night, of the seasons, of growth and decline, of life and death are those which are most apparent to us, but life itself—the development of species, races, civilizations—also presents the same cyclic character, of which the broadest aspect for us is the cycle of the four *yugas,* or four ages of humanity. These four ages lead to the almost total destruction of mankind, and then to its progress and new decline, during a cycle known as the *manvantara,* which lasts tens of thousands of years and in India is reckoned by the procession of equinoxes.

Within this general cycle, other shorter cycles develop, which see the rise and fall of civilizations as their peoples progress and decline with ineluctable regularity.

For mankind as a whole, we are now in the Fourth Age, the Age of Decline, which the Hindus call the Age of Conflicts (*Kali Yuga*).[1] This age will head increasingly swiftly toward the disruption of all values and will end in a catastrophe which will destroy mankind. According to the *Bhavishya Purana,* the "Chronicle of the Future," this catastrophe will take the form of an explosion under the sea. A kind of volcano, which the Sanskrit texts refer to

---

1. *Kali* means "quarrel," or "conflict" and should not be confused with *Kali,* the "power of time" (from *kala,* "duration").

as the "Mule's Head" (*Vadavamukha*), will erupt at the bottom of the sea and will destroy almost all life on the planet. Among the few survivors, there will then appear a new golden age, the Age of Truth (*Satya Yuga*), followed by the Ternary Age (*Treta Yuga*), after which comes the Age beyond the Two (*Dvapara Yuga*), and finally, the Age of Conflicts once more, with its catastrophic end. For five thousand years, we have been living in the Age of Conflicts that began at the time of the Mahabharata war, which saw the autochthones fight against the Aryan invaders. The end of mankind therefore appears to be relatively near.

The mankind we know, however, is not the first. Humanity has already appeared six times on the earth, developed, and reached the highest levels of technical and scientific progress, only to be destroyed in a general calamity. After us, mankind will rise and fall seven times more before the earth itself becomes an uninhabitable desert.

As we advance through the Age of Conflicts, our virtues deteriorate and are replaced with irresponsibility, corruption, and egoism. The sciences, originally the preserve of those who knew how to use them wisely, are given over to men who have not the discernment necessary to avoid their misuse. Instead of trying to realize fully his own nature and role in society, each man tries to take the place of others more qualified than he. In the resulting social disorder, hierarchies are based on ambition rather than efficacy. The good soldier becomes an odious tyrant, the good craftsman an incapable minister, the prince a corrupt businessman, the scholar a servile employee.

The interior and spiritual life becomes separated from knowledge, while religion becomes blind belief and an instrument of persecution. All the religions born during the Age of Conflicts have the same social revolutionary character, and their often aberrant dogmas serve as an instrument for the dominion of the temporal power. Only mystics, by isolating themselves from the world, know by intuition how to reestablish contact with eternal realities, but they are usually ignored or persecuted.

THE ORIGIN OF THE AGES, THE RACES, AND THE CASTES

The first men to appear at the beginning of the Age of Gold of a new era are the seers (*rishis*), sages who are still close to the gods. They are prodigious in intelligence, power, and virtue, and they procreate by the power of their thought alone, like the Cosmic Being. They have an immediate and intuitive perception of the laws that govern the world, some of which they codify for the use of future generations. All religions and all peoples share in some form this belief in ancient prophets who, through their superior intelligence and powers of divination, have been able to reveal truths and establish laws that are valid for all time to come. Such a belief, however twisted its later form may become, expresses an instinctive recognition of the reality of counterevolution or continuing deterioration of mankind on an interior level, if not on the material plane. The seers' role is like that of the gods, who assure the worlds' functions. These sages are thus a kind of intermediary, differing from the gods in that they live in the world of action (*karma*) and are subject to its laws. Their actions affect their future, which is the subtle source of human decline. Like them, the seers' sons are sages, whose tendency is toward a return to divine nonbeing, but they are maladjusted to their role as external witnesses of the divine play of creation.

Being able to visualize man's destiny, the sages have no desire to procreate, but to be reintegrated with the divine being from which they came forth. This does not accord with the plans of the gods, who use men as witnesses whose perception gives an appearance of reality to a world which is only a divine dream, an illusion without substance.

In order to make mankind multiply, the gods invented physical love and sent the *Apsaras*, the most beautiful and seductive of heaven's daughters, to divert the sages from their meditations and ascetic life and draw them into the cycle of transmigratory beings. Little by little, the sons of the sages allowed themselves to be tempted by the illusions of physical happiness, thus giving

22

birth to the first race of men, who were superior beings.

This succession of mythic events set in motion a cycle of four distinct phases of historical development known as the Four Great Ages. As has been mentioned, all of mankind's collective development is divided into four ages, beginning with the Age of Truth, or Golden Age (Satya Yuga), and ending with the present Age of Disorder and Conflict (Kali Yuga). According to Hindu concepts, all existence—whether individual or collective—is governed in all its forms by a similar fourfold division; thus, life itself always has four aspects. These four periods of development occur in the full lifetime of each one of us: childhood, youth, maturity, and old age. Each of these periods in Hindu philosophy is dominated by one of the four aims of life, which are virtue, success, pleasure, and liberation.

The first aim of life, virtue (*dharma*) is the art of behaving according to one's own fundamental qualities, and hence the observance of a code of conduct given by nature and birth. A king's virtues differ from those of a craftsman, and their implementation depends very largely on the education received as a child.

The second aim of life is achieved during youth by realization on the social level and the achievement of success, property, wealth, and power (*artha*).

The third aim of life is sensual pleasure (*kama*), whose fullness is enjoyed on the attainment of maturity.

The fourth aim, spiritual realization involving renunciation and leading to liberation (*moshka*), is dominant during the fourth stage of life, old age.

At no stage in life, however, can any of these aims be achieved if the others are neglected.

Human society is able to mature and stabilize when it is also divided into four main groups: the intellectual class (*Brahma*); the warrior class (*Kshatra*); the farming or merchant class (*Vaishya*); and the working class (*Shudra*), and it is this division that has given rise to the theory of caste. If creation is envisaged as being of divine origin, it appears logical that the various aptitudes of the different types of men correspond to the needs of society, as with bees, which have queens, drones, and workers. The four aims of life correspond to the four human types: the intellectuals, including the priestly class, seek moshka; the warriors (including kings), dharma; the farmers and merchants, artha; and the workmen, kama.

According to Hindu tradition, the four successive ages gave rise to the four creations or races of men, which are therefore at different stages of development corresponding to the four ages of life. The oldest, to which the priestly caste belongs, is said to be white. The second race, which includes warriors, nobles, and kings, is referred to as red. The third, the race of the farmers and merchants, is yellow, and the fourth, that of the artisan and workers, is black.

These four colors—white, yellow, red, and black—are considered in a symbolic or archetypal sense and are not directly equated with Caucasian, Oriental, or Negro but are related only in a wide analogical manner. A fourfold division of this symbolic form will take place naturally in any integrated societal organization, just as the four functional divisions of digestion, assimilation, circulation, and elimination occur in some form in all living organisms. For example, the very slightly lighter-skinned Bengali people from west-central India take the social role of the white race when integrated into the Dravidian Tamil society of South India. In some African societies the taller, darker-skinned people take the role of the white race in relation to pygmy populations. Each of these four colors denotes symbolically a composite of qualities, characteristics, or aptitudes—red, passionate and regal; black, deep and earthy; white, austere and pure; yellow, radiant and expansive—and these characteristics will enhance a functional activity in both biological as well as social organization.

Similarly, on an elemental level, oxygen, hydrogen, nitrogen, and carbon each carry specific observable qualities and must interact with one another according to laws and regularities in order for organic matter to form and grow. Likewise, the philosophical elements—earth, air, fire, and water—each demonstrate particular qualities and consistently affect and interact with each other in an archetypically patterned way. Society, based on the interplay of races and castes in the Hindu world, must also maintain a distinct functional clarity of interaction or fall into conflict and chaos.

THE FOUR STAGES OF BIOLOGICAL MATURATION	THE FOUR SOCIAL CASTES
Childhood Youth Maturity Old age	Shudra: artisan, worker Vaishya: farmer, merchant Kshatriya: aristocrat, warrior Brahmana: priest, scholar
THE FOUR HISTORICAL AGES	THE FOUR GOALS OF LIFE
Satya Yuga: Age of Truth Treta Yuga: Age of Ritual Dvapara Yuga: Age of Doubt Kali Yuga: Age of Conflict and Darkness	Dharma: virtue Artha: success Kama: pleasure Moksha: liberation
THE FOUR RACES OF HUMANITY	THE FOUR BODILY FUNCTIONS
Black Yellow Red White	Digestion Assimilation Circulation Excretion

Only judicious and appropriate conduct toward each caste and each race makes for peaceful coexistence and for the survival and refinement of each within its own limitations. It is evident that each race, having different characteristics and abilities, also has different duties, rights, and privileges. The balance of duties and privileges and the equitable distribution of advantages and pleasures constitute the fundamental condition for caste and race relations. Each race must have its social and human limitations and advantages, which cannot, however, be the same for the others. The musician needs his lute and the laborer his plough; the poet may need inebriation to give free rein to his muse; while the priest must take neither alcohol nor intoxicants for fear of making an error in the rites and thereby rendering them ineffective. The needs, duties, and rule of life are not the same for all.

The higher the rank of a human group, the more duties prevail over rights. The priest's asceticism and the knight's courage are not in themselves desirable for the other social groups, for whom wealth and pleasure are the aims of life.

There is no superior caste. The Universe is the work of the Immense Being. The beings created by him were only divided into castes according to their aptitude.
(Mahabharata, Shanti Parva, *188*)

We despise neither children nor old people, but if we were to treat them as we would a man in the prime of life and ignore the differences in their requirements, limitations, and strengths, we would clearly be doing them wrong. According to the Hindus, the misapprehension of the reality of age difference between the various human races leads to insoluble adjustment problems, and for many, it robs life of its true meaning. Young peoples cannot be treated like adults or like old peoples. Symbolically, children bring into the world the most intense forms of the qualities of sincerity, spontaneity, innocence, sensuality, and creativity, in contrast to the qualities of reason, precaution, and readiness to calculate the more mature stages of life. Likewise, the peoples that are growing old bring mankind their wisdom and knowledge, so long as they are not upset and destroyed by the activities of the younger peoples. Throughout history, down to our own times, we can see the sack of civilizations and the destruction of ancient peoples who should rather have been piously preserved and supported, just as the treasures of art and wisdom are preserved in our museums and libraries.

The division of the human species into different racial and social groups, with different aptitudes, ideals of life, and distinct modes of religious, artistic, and intellectual expression, is an ethnic fact which we can do nothing to change. The only safeguard for individual and social liberty consequently lies in the formation of multiple groups which, protecting each other from interference, allow all to live together under the same administration or in the same country, without conflict, without one group imposing its concepts, way of life, or morality on the others, and without even a clash of interests.

Each group must therefore have its independent sphere of activity, forbidden to the other groups.

The Hindu concept of attributing distinct advantages and restrictions to the various social groups has greatly facilitated race relations. An Indian shudra cursing his neighbor does not wish him to be reborn as an ass or a pig but as a Brahman, who can own nothing, cannot take another wife, and has not even the right to eat a good roast of lamb.

Must we consider that the characteristics of the various races of mankind, and in particular the color of their skin, are purely accidental, in a world developing wholly by accident and chance, or that these characteristics have been willed by the divinities involved and that they correspond to special abilities and to a definite role to be played in the world and in human society?

If the latter is so, the efforts of individuals belonging to a particular group to appropriate the functions of another group would be against nature, leading only to incompetence and social disorder. Hierarchies based on ambition, as they are envisaged by the Western world today, are profoundly artificial. Why should the profession of teacher or merchant be more desirable than that of the worker? It is a matter of nature, and the nature of each individual is determined from birth. Each man's duty, success in the world, and spiritual destiny all depend on his realization of what he really is and on his fulfilling his social role. The idea that one type of occupation is in itself nobler or more elegant than another is a concept that can appear only in a society whose values are perverted, where every soldier wants to be an officer. Such a situation inevitably leads to inefficiency and to class war, in which the only social morality appears to be the appropriation of someone else's place, without taking into any account individual aptitudes or the Creator's intentions.

The problem of social demands often arises not from the denial of real advantages to certain ethnic or social groups but rather from jealousy that would place in power persons who are incapable of wielding it for long, thus rapidly creating a far worse situation than before and dragging other social groups down together.

ELEMENTS OF SOCIAL ORDER

Collective organizations of animals and insects always revert to certain patterns and types of society. In order to understand how an ant acts, even when isolated from its habitual environment, we need some general knowledge about its usual form of society. Human society is not intrinsically different from animal societies; it merely appears more complex from certain points of view.

An ideal society must be based on the form of society that is natural to man and suited to his biological nature and collective psychology as a social being. All attempts at social reform that do not take sufficient account of man's individual and collective nature are doomed to failure. From the point of view of a systematic study of mankind's collective tendencies, it must be stated that most modern ideologies are mere abstractions—dreams corresponding to no possible form of real society. If biological facts and the differences between the sexes and races are ignored rather than harmonized, an artificial society is created in which practice fails to match theory. As a result, society is constantly plagued by conflict and disorders, which can be fatal, and inevitably becomes unjust and unhuman, since the more cunning rather than the more deserving will often appropriate every advantage.

When political or social theories ill-suited to man's nature are imposed by either force or persuasion, the results are always entirely different from their inventor's expectations. In the resulting social and political crises, entire civilizations can flounder and disappear unless an eventual reaction brings about a return to more normal social patterns.

None of the founders of the political and social systems currently discussed in the West seem to have studied the patterns of stable human societies. At their best, these systems are thus mere trends, which never lead to any durable form; they are abstractions, serving only to shake certain older social orders. They are not viable forms of human society, except perhaps in the case of very small, homogenous groups, whose political system requires simple conventional agreements, privately arranged among equals.

Ignorance of man's social nature leads to paradoxes, such as the class struggles in self-professed egalitarian societies, or wars of religion between groups proclaiming universal brotherhood. A stable society requires empirical observations, and not ideas, in building its foundation. At this point, we find that we know nothing of the natural order of human society, the pattern to which all societies inevitably return. Is human society matriarchal like that of the bees, or a tribe with an elective male chief like the deer? Is man naturally monogamous like the tiger, or polygamous like the monkey? Is he carnivorous like the wolf, or fruit-eating like the gorilla? Only a dispassionate, technical study of man's nature can lead to discovering his basic instincts and those of the various types of man, and subsequently to finding the bases of a society to suit everybody, in which each man can find the climate and form of life and activity that best suits him.

The Hindus assert that their social formula meets the requirements of man's individual and collective nature. The fact that the Hindu civilization has been able to survive over thousand of years, despite disorders caused by invasions, schisms, and internal wars, and has been capable of constant renewal, as demonstrated by one brilliant period after another, merits all our attention in the study of a social system whose longevity is unique in history.

Beginning with what is considered the historic period, there seem to have been two main kinds of human society according to race and origin: the tribe and the village, deriving from the nomadic and sedentary forms of society, which are patriarchal and matriarchal, respectively. These two kinds of natural society remain perpetually at the basis of our behavior patterns.

We retain the tribal mentality in many of our ways of thinking; for example, man always instinctively considers himself to be part of a group. At all levels, he creates groups, which he opposes violently to other similar groups. He proclaims himself French or

German, Christian or Muslim, Republican or Democrat. He feels the need to belong to a collective entity that opposes other entities with which he wants to fight, although his membership in one group or the other is usually quite accidental and the result of circumstances unaffected by free will or intelligence. This is particularly the case with religious membership, which is practically never the result of a well-reflected choice and yet is one of the fields in which fanaticism and intolerance are found in the most stupid, inhuman, and violent forms. Most men are ready to fight to defend ideas, organizations, and social orders whose value they have never questioned; this readiness to fight is characteristic of the elementary mentality of primitive tribes.

The other feature of human society is the village, which emerged as soon as divisions of work or specialization became necessary. People are thus not divided into independent groups but distributed in superimposed layers, sharing out the various functions of society. Whereas tribal organization always leads to separate and isolated groups, a stratified society gathers a certain number of ethnic groups into the same organization. The practical advantages of a stratified society are considerable, and indeed, no sedentary society of any importance has ever been developed without categories of individuals, or classes. There are, however, differences in the recruiting of the various classes as well as in the manner of apportioning social advantages, which are, in effect, the only real differences between societies. The form, stability, and harmony of the society all depend on the solution found for these arrangements. All societies whose institutions ignore the inevitable existence of social categories and the necessity to distribute advantages and assets among them, and in which the establishment of hierarchies is left to chance and intrigue, have inevitably ended with the oppression of some groups by others and with maladjustment, producing class struggles and the interminable chain of revolution.

The administrative divisions known as nations cut arbitrarily across the caste hierarchy and create communities with antisocial interests, inasmuch as they oppose the interests of one arbitrary group to those of another equally arbitrary group. Such communities are often strengthened in their isolation by developing linguistic and cultural units and forming habits of thought and expression, which ignore the similar or divergent habits of other groups. It is for this reason that nations easily become the victims of highly hermetic supranational castes, such as the multinational trading companies of our time.

These principles serve as a basis for Hindu society is an attempt to create a stable polity, acknowledging the necessity for stratified divisions while seeking to accord an equitable position for each group, so that each receives equivalent though different privileges to match the varying responsibilities, duties, and functions.

Prior to colonial intervention, the resulting corporative organization created a deep unity over a continent whose linguistic, racial, religious, and national extremes and divisions seemed to condemn it to perpetual discord. It created harmony in which differences of origin were attenuated by the unity of the occupational group. Clashes between the different peoples were reduced to a kind of folklore competition, in which each was proud of being different, and to tournaments between princes to win noble titles. These activities no longer affected the continuation of civilization and the right of each class of individuals and ethnic and religious groups to stay as they were, keeping their customs, religion, social life, and systems of marriage and inheritance without impeding those of others. In fact, the differences in dress, custom, and manners became a title of glory and interest instead of an object of scorn and ridicule by groups who considered themselves superior or more evolved.

The corporative society has been instrumental in transforming tribal autonomy into interactive competition and in directing interest toward group improvement instead of isolation and avoidance between neighboring groups. Competitive sports and folk dances serve a similar purpose for the West, but to a more limited extent, whereas the Hindus' social system has carried this attitude into every aspect of life.

In Europe during the Middle Ages, such corporations were also known in the form of guilds, together with all the advantages that this type of organization makes possible, since the corporation is a world in itself rather like a tribe or nation. It has its notables, technicians, experts, apprentices, festivals, and ceremonies, and is conscious of the values it represents in relation to other social groups.

In India, corporative privileges include the right to make laws and administer justice. Each caste can establish its own rules for marriage, divorce, and inheritance, and in each city or village elects its own "Council of Five" (*panchayat*), which passes judgement on all differences concerning the group as well as on minor offenses that do not affect other groups (those that do are the responsibility of the State). In both his private and collective life, therefore, a man can be judged only by his peers, since what is forbidden in one caste may very well be permitted in another. Questions such as adultery, divorce, bigamy, incest, prostitution, homosexual relationships, the division of property, debts, loans, the use of intoxicants, public drunkenness, and riots are settled by the panchayat, which is much better qualified to understand the group's problems and conventions than a judge and lawyers of another caste. Furthermore, the panchayat brooks no delays and costs nothing.

Problems such as drugs, whether harmless or dangerous, minor thefts and offenses, which our society finds insoluble, are more easily resolved by panchayats of students or workers. The differences between a working-class and a middle-class jury in estimating the same crime, as mentioned by Kinsey, clearly show the advantage of being judged by one's peers. Only they can know whether the accused was conscious of committing a serious offense, since moral concepts differ for each caste and no law can be valid for all.

THE CASTES

The institution we know as the caste system is called *varna-ashrama* for the Hindus, *varna* meaning color, and *ashrama* a refuge of peace and harmony. The aim of the system is thus the harmonious coexistence of the various races and different sorts of human beings.

From its very beginning, the caste system was envisaged as the expression and codification of the social and ethnic realities inherent in all societies. The Hindu lawgivers felt that no advanced society could exist without the recognition of certain facts, such as professional organizations; relations between the various occupations needed to maintain the economic, political, and social stability of the state; and the problems arising from the various degrees of development among peoples and individuals, their various aptitudes, and the drawbacks of intermarriage. It should not be forgotten that the so-called equality in aptitude of the sundry human races takes only the capacities of the most aggressive races into account, and not of those that are unable to adapt to modern conditions, such as the Pygmies, the Australian aborigines, the munda populations of India, and many other groups. Their systematic genocide still continues today, since their existence upsets all ideas of so-called equality of aptitude, values, and aspirations among the various races. For the Hindus, the caste system is not a man-made invention to justify slavery but the recognition of the Creator's will, the codification of a state of fact, an attempt to harmonize human society in accordance with the general scheme of creation.

The division of society into castes is thus based on three main elements found unfailingly in all societies: race, profession, and ethics. Personal ethics always lie outside the scope of collective values and relate only to the individual's inner self-improvement. The particular aptitudes of the various races, the professions that permit their full exploitation, and the codes of conventions or ethics form the basis of all societies.

It is easy to see that despite all the national and linguistic barriers, even modern Western society is fundamentally, like all societies, a caste system. From whatever position we view it, we see international corporations whose members have far more in common with each other than with the various professional or social levels of their own country.

We speak, for example, of the claims of the working classes, who rightly demand economic or cultural advantages. Skilled workers are craftsmen and rarely wish to change profession and become teachers, priests, or soldiers. They are proud of their technical abilities in areas in which those of other social groups are incompetent or inefficient. The problems of Western society derive from the fact that while proclaiming the equality of men, it is entirely graded on a hierarchical system as far as the professions are concerned.

Members of every professional group have wider affinities and deeper and more constant contacts with the other members of the group or caste than with any other group. At this point another caste element intervenes: race. Even within the most tightly knit professional group, barriers are raised against extraneous ethnic elements whose habits, ways of thinking and acting, and codes of ethics are different. This is not a matter of habit or education but of nature and is therefore inevitable and necessary if each man is to realize himself according to his own nature and avoid the frustrations and deformations that arise in adopting the customs of another race.

This phenomenon reappears periodically, occasionally with great violence. The powers of kings and the creation of empires have often replaced ethnolinguistic groups with much larger organizations, grouping together for administrative purposes different elements that must either be assimilated, subjugated, or destroyed. Only the recognition of ethnic differences by society's laws and organization can allow the various associated groups to maintain their autonomy, originality, and racial purity.

Under the pretext of equality, Western lawmakers do not let the various groups cooperate among themselves while keeping their different habits, ethics, and social life. Jews, Mormons, Muslims, Celts, Basques, Albigensians, Pygmies, blacks, or Inuits are accorded a relative equality only on condition that they conform to our customs, losing most of their social, national, and religious characteristics and in fact abandoning their own personality. In order to cope with all the problems posed by a multiracial society, the

Hindu lawgivers sought to establish rules making coexistence possible, resulting in the caste system which is still today solidly established in India despite all efforts to destroy it.

In a country where populations of highly different origins and aptitudes live side by side, from men of the forest to refined Gangetic craftsmen and proud Aryan warriors, an equitable place had to be found for all. Each had to be able to continue in his ancestral way of life, governed by laws suited to him and with the form of social, religious, agricultural, intellectual, and moral life he preferred, without adversely affecting the rest of the community. This meant recognizing each group and each individual's right to be different, which is in fact liberty's only valid criterion.

The first step toward this aim was a profound study of the human species and the nature of the requirements of the individual and of civilized society, in order to reach a compromise that would take into account the individual and collective nature of human beings. The first questions to be asked were these: What is man? What are the characteristics of social man? Are there divisions within the human species like those of the ants and the bees? If they exist, are these divisions biological or social? Are man's characteristics inherited or acquired, or both? Can a developed society be established without these divisions? How can the needs of the individual or the group be compatible with those of the larger society?

Their observation of social phenomena and of individual and group psychology led the law-making philosophers of India to the conclusion that man is not an isolated instance in the natural order, and that consequently certain cosmological and metaphysical concepts can be applied to human society just as they apply to all other manifestations—astronomy, mathematics, physical substances, plants, animals. The resulting social concepts are the fruit of a conscious examination of the natural world and a desire to conform with the mind of the Creator. The visible world, as the materialization of the Creator's thought, expresses a divine internal harmony. We ourselves approach the divine and the real by perceiving and cooperating with this harmony, in which lies the essence of morality. It is by means of this path that we can attain the goals of life. If man inwardly and outwardly participates in the Creator's work, he can draw nearer and nearer until he indentifies himself in him. This is the sublime privilege of man's estate. Consciousness and free will give man's actions a magical value which neither the angels nor the animals possess, making him the fulfillment and crown of creation, the point at which the creature, freed from the chains of the created, can by the power of his intelligence and the force of his actions identify himself anew with his Creator.

Such freedom, however, can lead to confusion and disorder, in which man loses his sense of destiny and mission. In order to fulfil his inner task, the external framework of his activities must conform as far as possible with the divine plan. The Hindu lawmakers believed that the diversity of races, hierarchy of castes, and variety of occupations, were an expression of human nature and a reflection of the divine scheme which man must seek to understand and to which he has every interest to conform, since only by this means can he attain his fulfillment and realize the four aims of life.

Every society is necessarily divided into four groups, corresponding to the four main functions without which no civilization can survive. The four divisions of human society, giving rise to the four castes, are defined in the Hindu system as follows:

1. Spiritual and intellectual authority, Brahma, represented by the priest-scholar caste, the *Brahmans.*
2. Executive or royal power of a moral and military nature, *Kshatra,* generally represented by the aristocracy of *kshatriyas,* or nobles, and warriors.
3. A commercial and financial class, whether bourgeois or agricultural, *Visha,* mainly represented by the farmers and merchants, the *vaishyas.*
4. The laborers' and artisans' class, called *Shudra.*

As with the four ages of life, the four castes reflect the four ages of humanity, and one of the aims of life dominates in each caste. This is why eroticism predominates in the workers' caste, property and money in the merchants' caste, courage and duty in the royal caste, and spiritual and intellectual life in the sacerdotal caste.

The initiation of an adolescent into the rites of his caste is considered a second birth,[2] since in the first three castes a long training is required before he can fulfill his duties and become an adult and a citizen. Shudras have no initiation as such, but only professional degrees in their craft, and are considered children throughout their life. This is why "Brahmans, Kshatriyas, and Vaishyas form the three castes of the twice-born. The fourth, the Shudra, has only one birth. There is no fifth caste" (*Manu*, 10.4).

Within each caste, according to the aptitude of its members, four subcastes are formed, subdivided into numerous categories corresponding to independent corporate, racial, religious, and professional groupings. Furthermore, in each group, the division of labor according to individual aptitude also reflects the division of the castes. There are thus intellectual shudras and Brahman workmen, but these subdivisions remain in the realm of individual ability and present no hereditary characteristics. When a warrior is ungifted in the military arts, his son does not lose caste and may well rediscover his ancestral aptitudes. Brahmans who have no bent for study often work as cooks, since everyone can receive food from their hands because of their very strict rules of ritual purity and hygiene.

The caste corresponds essentially to a function, a profession reserved for a corresponding type of individual. Once the relationship is established between the group and the function, it is maintained by racial selection, together with special forms of education, eating habits, customs, and ethics, which differ from group to group, so as to favor the individual's specialization.

OCCUPATION, HEREDITY, ENVIRONMENT

The more advanced and civilized a society, the greater the need for specialists. To this end, it is clearly profitable for certain individual

---

2. The Christian sacrament of confirmation is a vestige of these rites.

characteristics to be accentuated in order to obtain maximum gain in every sphere of activity. If all children are reared in the same manner up to a certain age, it will be to the detriment of their professional training and thus of their social usefulness. It is nearly impossible to make a good acrobat, horseman, linguist, or sailor without training from childhood. All professions requiring specialized training already have a caste system, each with its own particular environment and history. Even if the value of heredity is doubted and the differences between individual aptitudes are attributed to environment, it becomes yet one more reason for establishing from childhood an environment that will the better adapt a person for a particular social occupation. The family profession is thus the best of all arrangements. It is well known that a horse that has pulled a cart will never make a racehorse. This very specialization, which allows the individual to attain a perfection of his type and which is so widely acknowledged as being necessary for animals, is in many cases denied to man.

The ideal of associating certain virtues with certain occupations is naturally hard to reach, but the very existence of this ideal implies that a man belonging to a certain caste feels that he has seriously failed if he neglects the duties of his estate.

The duties of a priest, the virtues of a king, the obligations of a knight form a context which, if borne in mind from childhood, largely become a part of the individual's character. For this reason, the various castes are defined in terms of duties, never of rights.

> *The system of the four castes was created by me according to the difference in aptitude and occupation. I created it, I who am inactive and immutable.*
>
> (Bhagavad Gita, 4.13)

> *He in whom you observe truth, charity, absence of enmity, modesty, goodness and austerity, is a Brahman.*
>
> *He who fulfils the duties of a knight, studies the holy books, dedicates his life to acquiring and distributing wealth, is a Kshatriya.*
>
> *He who loves husbandry, agriculture and money, who is*

honest and instructed in the holy books, is a Vaishya.
He who eats anything, undertakes any profession, does
not observe the rules of purification, and is not interested
in the holy books or rules of life, is a Shudra.
(Mahabharata, Shanti Parva, *ch. 149)*

Caste in Hindu society is thus at once racial, familial, religious, and professional, characterized by systems that differ for each caste: racial selection (marriage with different degrees of consanguinity), education, dietary laws (vegetarian or non-vegetarian), and codes of ethics. The result is that intercaste marriage and certain social relations are forbidden, particularly meals taken in common, since the various groups have different dietary laws. In principle, this system allows races with different endowments to develop their aptitudes for their different professions and enhances the role of racial minorities in national life, since there is probably no race that is not clearly superior on at least one level, which needs only to be identified and utilized. In the Hindu system, each caste also has its own ethical code, social system, and rules of hygiene adapted to its social level and occupation.

As an example, one of the dark-skinned pre-Aryan peoples, the ancient Abhiras (now called Ahirs) form the caste of cattle-breeders and dairymen and are met with in every town in India. They are strong and highly erotic and play an essential role in society. They have kept their own institutions, customs, and music, which have no relation with those of any other ethnic group. They form an artisanal caste of Shudras and are proud of their origins and their profession. Nothing would induce them to abandon their originality, seek another occupation, or mix with other castes.

To some modern eyes, to be destined from birth to a certain profession is an injustice, to which it can be objected that all professions are indispensable and that one is as good as another. However the selection is performed, there will always be a difference or inequality between professional groups. The real problem consists in making all professions honorable, rather than in opening to everyone certain professions considered more respectable than others. In fact, it is when a man of value performs a humble job that he most deserves honor. An intelligent man can always use his faculties and serve his country by developing his family profession. To obtain a high level of technical progress in all branches of national activity, it is of the greatest importance that the most gifted individuals do not all abandon the humble professions in favor of others that are thought to be elegant or profitable and would thus become overcrowded.

The *Bhagavad Gita* says, "Never leave the family profession, even if it has drawbacks."

Although other societies may determine caste by other means, hereditary caste is much the simplest form of selection, since the two elements of heredity and environment tend to orient the individual toward his family occupation from childhood.

This is not only the case in India. Even in the Western world, a young man often takes up his father's profession. The son of a solicitor often becomes a solicitor.

There is a way in Hindu society, however, for particularly gifted individuals to leave their caste, although this can only be done on a personal basis, not on a social level or for purposes of material gain. The exceptional individual is entitled to a place of honor only if he abstains from procreation. He may therefore renounce marriage and family life and wear the monastic robe of the *sannyasi,* who is outside and above all castes. He may also devote himself to the study of science, arts, letters, or philosophy, even while staying with his family, but he may not make it his profession nor draw his family or children away from the family occupation. Many of the great Indian poets, mystics, artists, and musicians belonging to the workers' caste have seen kings prostrate themselves before them. Princes, too, have been musicians and painters, but without making art their profession or abandoning their knightly duties.

In the Hindu religion, the life of the sannyasi does not involve being cloistered in a monastery. Bound only by vows (which do not necessarily include chastity), the sannyasi lives free and often plays a very active role in political, religious, or intellectual life, since it is his duty to teach philosophy, ethics, and theology in every village he passes through. It is forbidden to ask a sannyasi the slightest question about his origins, caste, or family. His ties with them no longer exist.

The possibility of changing their profession must be clearly open to exceptional individuals who wish to change. However, we should not lose sight of the fact that people have the basic right to continue their family profession, not—as we are sometimes asked to believe—that everyone has a right to all professions. This destruction of dynasties of craftsmen to the profit of industry has created a lack of interest in work, an uncertainty in the face of life that is the curse of the young in the Western world. Their supposed freedom of choice is in fact only too often a baited trap, which allows us to attribute the most flagrant social injustice to bad luck or chance and thus free ourselves of the obligation to remedy it. Under the pretext that badly paid workers have only to look for another job, we no longer feel obliged to deal with the claims and problems of a particular social or ethnic group unless it is strong enough to disturb our comfort by means of strikes.

THE FOUR TYRANNIES

Any attempt to create a stable society and reduce the dominance of one group over another that inevitably leads to war and destruction must arrive at a form of government based on a caste system. This must, in particular, include the creation of a spiritual authority, completely independent of the executive or royal power and superior to them. Economic and financial life inevitably becomes the province of a specialized class, while the workers, divided into corporations, possess inalienable rights and a large portion of the wealth of the state. Such a division of society produces stability. If any one group oversteps its rights to the detriment of others, it automatically faces a coalition of the other three and is easily led to cooperate.

Students (intellectuals) and workers uniting to fight the merchants and warriors can only be entrapped and get nowhere, whereas the three groups uniting against a fourth that oversteps its limits are sure of success.

Outside the caste system, which assures a balance between the essential functions of any society, there has never existed, nor can there exist, any system that does not lead to the tyrannical supremacy of one of the castes or social categories. Thus, according to Manu, there are four types of tyrannical government: dictatorship by the clergy, dictatorship by the aristocracy, dictatorship by the bourgeousie, and dictatorship by the proletariat. Although differing in form, these four types of government are similar in nature and are equally unstable and unjust. None of them can last because they are based on domination by a single caste, which must oppress or crush the others in order to remain in power. This can never succeed, since, suppressed from outside, the same inevitable divisions and inequalities reappear within the dominant class itself, recommencing the eternal race for power.

In none of these forms of government is there a law above and beyond the interests, ideas, and beliefs of the group in power. Thus, no one can assure the other groups of their right to be different or to have the religion, ethical code, and civilization that suit them. All dictatorships, whether of the proletariat, the army, the bourgeoisie, or the church live by means of propaganda, brainwashing, oppression, prisons, and the stake, whose very horror often escapes their authors because they believe they are different from members of other castes. Even under bourgeois dictatorship (i.e., by capitalists of the merchant class), the prisons are full of people belonging to the working class, who are there for petty theft or other minor and insignificant crimes. Meanwhile, the quasi-legal "appropriations" of the business world are treated with benevolence (the law being made for them and by them), although a single one of their malpractices may well be worth far more than the combined crimes of thousands of working-class prisoners.

Only the caste system, which is somewhat similar to the medieval European social structure comprising guilds, clergy, bourgeoisie, and princes, has sufficient authority to control the government in power, whether bourgeois or military (royal). The difficulty lies in placing the arbiters of the law beyond any corruption, influence, or violence. For this reason, in Hindu society, the Brahmans' rule of life is strict, shaping their character from childhood with a rigidity that the Spartans or the samurai might well envy. At the same time, their social position is unassailable, and the putting to death of a Brahman is forbidden by the most terrible sanctions. In practice, all technical or money-making professions are forbidden to the Brahman except the priesthood and teaching, and even then he may not sell his knowledge or teach for pay. This is why traditional scholars in modern India cannot teach in European-style universities, since professors are salaried employees who sell their knowledge without being able to consider whether their students are qualified to receive it or avoid its misuse.

The establishment of a world order that is stable and just and allows each individual to fulfil the four aims of life involves returning to a form of society that recognizes the realities of race and caste, in order to implement a social structure that prevents any one race or caste from encroaching on the others or oppressing or destroying them.

Far from guiding the world toward an ideal future for human society, democratic ideas are probably no more than a brief period of romantic politics, which will lead the world into great turmoil. The social and political ideologies of the modern West will probably appear as childish and absurd to our descendants as they seem irresponsible and incoherent to traditionalist Hindus today.

RACE AND RACISM

The respect accorded by the caste system to the various races and cultures is exactly the contrary of what the West terms racism. Racism, whose logical outcome is genocide, is the defense system of an oligarchy that claims to be superior and egalitarian. The naive and romantic social ideas of Europeans who preach the equality of man but insist that equality must be on the level of their own beliefs, way of life, customs, clothing, feeding habits, hygiene, and so on can only lead to genocide or false assimilation, which will in the end destroy the society that fathered it. To present the Pygmies or Mundas of India with the alternatives of becoming bankers, lawyers, or factory workers, or else of disappearing, is a sinister jest, which has unfortunately already justified the annihilation of many human races. In the whole of history, India has been the only defender of peoples who do not adapt to the industrial exploitation of the world. The nomadic gypsies, victims of racism in Europe, have never had problems in India since their expulsion from their original home in Gandhara (present-day Afghanistan) by Islamized Arab, Turkish, and Mongol invaders. Anti-Jewish racism is first and foremost a struggle for economic and financial supremacy, directed against the only people in the West who resisted the imposition of Christianity. In India, the Jews form a caste and have never known such problems.

DUTIES AND PRIVILEGES

It is clearly not feasible to create a society in which all individuals or groups have the same rights or privileges. However, it is possible for the members of each caste to enjoy the rights they would have in a society dominated by themselves. Thus, the bourgeoisie and the workers do not have the same way of life, but the bourgeois can indeed enjoy the rights and privileges he would have in a bourgeois society, and the workers the way of life that would be theirs in a proletarian state. The desire to deprive others of what one cannot have oneself, or does not want to have, is morally indefensible and fundamentally antisocial.

In the Hindu caste system, the more privileges a certain class enjoys, the more it is restricted by duties and limitations. The case of high-caste individuals who wish to enjoy all the privileges of their rank without fulfilling any of its duties or observing the restrictions on their behavior is, curiously enough, entirely the creation of the Muslim and Christian conquerors, who, believing that they were protecting the individual against caste tyranny, in fact allowed unscrupulous people to harm the collectivity with impunity, by preventing the application of sanctions against them

44

and against the abuse and accumulation of privileges.

It is certain that abusive caste practices were introduced when the administrative power ceased to be in Hindu hands, thus making the repression of abuses legally impossible. Many of the current Indian leaders were educated abroad, and observe only those traditional rules of life that are to their advantage. Consequently, they can no longer be considered Hindus.

Such abuses as there are have been greatly exaggerated in order to justify Western domination and are normally quite local. In most of India, the caste system functions today as it always has: as a harmonious whole in which each is satisfied with his social lot, in which the freedom of each tribe, family, and religious group to live according to its customs, traditions, and convictions is respected as it is in no other country and no other form of society. Even in modern India, the most humble artisan, like the craftsman of medieval Europe, is proud of his race, profession, caste, and customs, which he would not want to exchange for anything in the world. Nor has he the slightest desire to impose his habits or ways of seeing things on others. Even if, like the Christian, he is convinced of the grounds of his religion, customs, and moral concepts, unlike the Christian he has no urge to proselytize because he realizes that he belongs to another race and a different culture from those of other castes, and he seeks to fulfil his own moral duty, which is not necessarily the same as for others.

CASTE AND MARRIAGE

The main problem affecting relations between castes and races is marriage. For the Hindu lawmaker, marriage is above all a social institution, whose exclusive purpose is the propagation of the species and preservation of the caste, community, and even the nation itself.

The Hindu makes a clear distinction between erotic enjoyment in all its forms, which is part of the harmonious development of the individual, and marriage, whose sole aim is the family and the continuation of the species. Marriage results not from love but from careful choice, which takes account only of the heredity, stability, and happiness of the children.

Momentary pleasures do not require an institution such as marriage, which can only lose dignity if viewed in such a light. Marriages of love, chance, or accident, which can be broken by divorce, as is countenanced today by many Westerners, are from the Hindu point of view absurd and immoral, a sort of legalized prostitution. The Western notion of marriage has no moral or social counterpart in Hindu society. Marriage is not merely the legitimizing of sexual relations but an important institution, whose exclusive purpose is offspring—the continuation of the species under the best possible conditions of heredity and environment.

Love with all its fantasies is an essential achievement for the individual, but marriage is quite different. The sexophobic fanaticism of the Christian world and its extraordinary taboos were needed to give a sacred character to a marriage in which the child's heritage is not even considered. The prohibition of interracial marriage has nothing to do with the supposed superiority or inferiority of certain races, which are all equally perfect, but with distinct physical and mental characteristics.

The acceptance of marriage in which the child is not the final purpose is matched in the Christian world by the persecution of freedom to love, of prostitution, and of homosexuality, which are an essential counterpart of family stability, of the homogenous couple and their offspring. It is only in modern times that Hindu parents had to bestow their children in marriage arragements because the laws of the invaders allowed marriages which were aberrant from the point of view of the races and castes.

The recognition of so-called love marriages between different races and castes gives religious and social sanction to what may appear as irresponsibility toward the future children. The institution of marriage on such a basis has no meaning, and the consequent systematic mismatching of aptitudes is producing an ever-increasing number of ill-adapted beings in the modern Western world, lacking the basic virtues of the various groups.

Based on respect for the species as the work of the Creator, marriage as an institution concerns caste, race, profession, and nation, with which the individual has no right to tamper because it affects everyone else. Divorce is allowed only for the workers' caste, whose laws are different and include the privilege of virtual freedom from sexual taboos.

If marriage restrictions are rigidly obeyed by all, the various castes or races can live amicably together, profiting by each other without endangering each other's customs, traditions, and progeny. Women in ancient India were never shut away as they were after the Muslim invasion and are even today, because they were respected by all, and marriage out of the caste was unthinkable. Only since the arrival of the Muslims and then of the Christians, who permitted interracial marriage, has the Hindu woman lost many liberties outside the home. Hindu legislation is not puritanical and gives much leeway to human weakness, but marriage outside the caste is considered an antisocial act jeopardizing the entire structure on which society is balanced.

At this point, the moral laws of the modern West and India are entirely different. Whereas in the West any union is moral if legalized, however dissimilar the partners, without any concern for future children, the Hindu considers the love marriage or marriage out of caste highly immoral and socially more dangerous than any kind of temporary liaison, including prostitution, homosexuality, and other sexual variants. Such temporary liaisons concern only individual morality, which is hardly touched by legislation; such legislation would be tyrannical, since the state is justified in restricting individual freedom only when there is a danger to innocent third parties (the progeny) and consequently to society.

The Hindu lawmakers were convinced that the mixing of castes or races largely destroys the moral value of the two parties in creating a primitive human material without the virtue of either group, which must be fashioned anew and formed over the centuries until this new alloy becomes homogeneous and can give birth to a new civilization or race with its own characteristics. Mixed races usually form a barrier, profoundly separating the two parent races and rarely serving to draw the two together.

However, friendship can be enjoyed with people of any race or caste, if all possibility of marriage is excluded but erotic relations are not excluded, to the mutual benefit of the persons involved. From the Hindu point of view, abstaining from out-of-caste marriage is as much a matter of basic social decency as refraining from making propositions to every woman in the street. In fact, the question is almost the same in both cases; it is differentiated only by the perspective of time. A passing adventure is immoral to the extent that it endangers family life, whereas intercaste marriage affects the life of a race, a caste, a thousand-year-old civilization. Such a marriage makes no sense, because marriage is only a link in the transmission of life, an instant in the life of a race or a dynasty. A procreative union that jeopardizes the organization of the life of a species is in itself far more antisocial and immoral than a momentary liaison without consequences.

CASTE AND DIET

Questions of custom, food, and religious practice play an important role in the theory of caste. Few people realize that a large majority of Hindus are meat-eaters. At the same time, some communities not only abstain from all meat but even observe severe restrictions over the vegetable products they may assimilate. Such dietary differences are not merely arbitrary and conventional but express a coherent theory based on the properties of the various foods and their ability to accentuate the physical and mental characteristics of the individual, the better to suit him for the duties of his caste and thus make him a more efficient and useful citizen.

No dietary restrictions can exist without a prohibition on castes eating with other castes. This prohibition is the sole guarantee that the individual, whether rich or poor, free or dependent, can take his proper nourishment, and it is largely in order to protect this freedom that caste laws have to be so strict.

CASTE AND CONQUEST

There is no moral objection to a prince or a state conquering other territories or peoples, providing caste restrictions and the duties of the conqueror are observed. By usurping the prerogatives of other castes, one becomes a tyrant. The conqueror has a perfect right to enjoy the fruits of his conquests, but as a knight, or Kshatriya. He may levy taxes and exact tribute, but should he use his military position to impose his language, religion, culture, or customs, he will be breaking the laws of caste. His empire will not endure, because conflicts will inevitably break out.

It was this error that led to the failure of all the Western colonial empires. The use of Christianity spread by missionaries as a means of assimilating conquered peoples has had disastrous results on every side. A conqueror's duties are clearly defined by Hindu law:

He must consider as law whatever the religion of the (conquered) peoples ordains. (Manu, 7.203)

Whatever the ethics, customs and family institutions of the conquered country, it is according to them that the country must be governed. (Yajñavalkya Smriti)

Mahatma Gandhi's use of the theory of nonviolence as a political weapon did not spring from Hindu tradition. Non-violence, to the Hindu, is a strictly individual technique for personal improvement and may not be used for political ends or play any role in the government of the state.

The whole of the *Bhagavad Gita* is, in fact, an admonition to Arjuna, who wished to renounce violence, thus failing in his duty as a prince and a soldier. With his theories of nonviolence, Gandhi might be viewed as the instrument of the massacres on an almost unprecedented historical scale that preceded and followed the partition of India.

The Outcastes

India has always had a problem with a certain number of outcastes, whose origin can be attributed to three main causes:

1. Individuals rejected by their caste for misconduct.
2. Nonassimilated foreign groups or primitive tribes.
3. Persons whose professions are considered unclean or who may not mix with others.

Much has been said and written about the pariahs, or outcastes of India, whereas in fact genuine outcastes are extremely rare and belong to the first category. They are, as it were, prisoners on parole, rather like excommunicates during the Middle Ages. The other untouchables form groups quite like other artisan castes but are subject to a few additional restrictions, especially concerning the use of wells.

Nothing, however, prevents such groups from developing economically and intellectually. A Parsi millionaire in Bombay has no more right than an aborigine from Orissa to draw water from a Brahman's well. Clearly, such a fact is more easily noticed in one case than in the other.

All persons born outside the Hindu world are untouchables, a fact that applies to all foreigners, and physical contact with them must be avoided. The problem of untouchability, however, has been poorly presented. It is the Brahman who cannot touch anyone because of his sacred functions and obligations of ritual purity. He is thus avoided respectfully by all, so as not to impose on him constant and difficult purificatory rites and even long fasts.

When a group adopts a new religion whose customs and rites are different from those of their original caste, a new caste is created for which an occupation and a place in society must be sought. This was the case with the Sikhs, who recruited their members from among the warrior castes, and also with the Christians, who mostly belong to the workers' caste or to pariah families. Apart from their military profession, the Sikhs were allotted several jobs, such as cart drivers (nowadays taxi drivers) while the Christians were unofficially given jobs as railway employees. The Sikhs, moreover, have given India many great ministers, ambassadors, and other leaders.

No society exists without its pariahs. Indeed, racial prejudice in certain Western countries has led to more violent segregation than India has ever known. In India there have never been ghettos like that of the Arabs in Paris or the Turks in Berlin. The persecution or exclusion of racial, religious, or other minorities is in fact crueller in the West, where persons of any level of development are vulnerable to attack, whether they are scholars, intellectuals, soldiers, merchants, or workers. Although Hindu law may exclude its pariahs and other castes from certain social contacts, it is never guilty of persecuting, converting, or isolating them, or of depriving them of work or public entertainment. On the contrary, the law immediately locates for them a place in society, sets aside an occupation, and creates festivals, dignities, and responsibilities for them.

Once the limits of each individual's relations with society have been established, he is not subject to any constraint or harassment. Respect for personal liberty and the right of every human being to be himself are acknowledged as the very basis of society by the Hindu world. This is perhaps a lesson that the Western world might learn.

When an individual is placed outside his normal social group by a special vocation or by accident, his moral nature, duties, and dharma become different, and he must then seek to realize his new nature fully and perfect himself through it. Although it is useless for the individual to try to be reintegrated into a group from which he has already been excluded, he may well be integrated into another group. Thus, a woman who has had a lover or has been raped is no longer fit for her role as mother because the heredity of her children is believed to be affected. There is no question of reproach, or of cruelty or scorn toward her, but merely of noting a state of fact, as if she had an incurable illness. Henceforth she will belong to the corporation of women who have had relations with several men, i.e., prostitutes, and her duties will be those of that group. She may choose the monastic life, or she may train herself

51

in the necessary arts and give herself unreservedly and freely to Brahmans, fulfilling the social role of her new profession as best she can. Just as she would have done in her original caste, she will thus perfect herself and draw near to that spiritual realization which is the final goal of all life. A very important chapter of the *Matsya Purana* explains the duties of a woman in such a situation.[3]

The same applies to those who have broken other prohibitions, such as eating beef or crossing the sea (in the case of a Brahman). Such people may no longer take their meals with others of their group or marry within it. From the Hindu point of view, almost all the Europeanized society of New Delhi that today governs India is a society of pariahs—a fact that often explains their vindictive hostility toward the traditional institutions that have rejected them.

PROTECTION OF LESS ADVANCED RACES

The caste system is often presented as a tyranny of the upper classes and is condemned as being contrary to social justice. However, if the caste system is viewed from the broad perspective of history, it is difficult not to arrive at different conclusions. Hindu society is reproached for the way it treats certain workers' castes and aboriginal tribes, keeping them at a distance and limiting social contacts with the rest of society to professional relations. Few realize that this is the only way in which certain races and very ancient forms of culture and religion can survive and even prosper in a world so alien to their own.

The sad tale of so many races whose faculties of adaptation were less developed than those of their conquerors, and who have vanished in the wake of more advanced civilizations, should give pause for thought. The rapid disappearance of such people as the Polynesians, the Australian aborigines, the American Indians, and certain African tribes could have been avoided if an intelligent

---

3. See A. Daniélou, *La Sculpture érotique hindoue* (Paris, 1973), pp. 71–73.

caste system had protected their customs, way of life, social system, and religion, and had allocated territories and professions to them, instead of pretending to want to assimilate them into a civilization requiring a different level of development from their own and thus assuring their extinction.

In the Hindu world, many races, civilizations, and religious and social systems have lived side by side in harmony and mutual respect for thousands of years, each individual assured of his means of livelihood and sphere of activity. The system of easily followed restrictions prevents one caste or race from encroaching on the others and from borrowing their religious rites, customs, ethical code, and system of inheritance or property.

Like all systems, the caste system can give rise to abuses. This has particularly been the case of the Indian colonies in southern India and in Bengal, not originally part of the sacred territory of the Hindus, which covered only the Indus and Ganges valleys. When these peoples, whose religion was either animism or ancient Shaivism and to whom the caste system was unknown, were included in the Hindu world, Brahman families from the north of India were sent there. Those families have since remained quite aloof from the rest of the population and even today are often extremely arrogant. This has given rise to incidents, whose importance has often been exaggerated. A Tamil national autonomist movement in South India demands the expulsion of the Brahmans from the administration, even though they have been established in the land for more than a thousand years.

Society's divisions, which are an unavoidable reality, become all the more cruel and unjust when they are ignored, and they reappear whatever theoretical, socialistic, or other principles are applied. Living conditions like those of the slums of Paris or New York are unthinkable in the traditional Hindu system, in which each ethnic group and each profession, however humble, has its rights and privileges. Such conditions appear only in the hybrid framework of the Western-type modern industrial cities in India.

Part Two

3 THE NATURE OF THE WORLD

THE NATURE OF THE WORLD

Before dealing with the detailed organization of human life as envisaged by the Hindus, it will be necessary to put man back into the context of Creation, since it is only by understanding man's reason for being and his function within the framework of creation that we can understand the meaning of his life and destiny realistically and not according to a utopian ideal.

According to Hindu philosophers, we perceive the world through duration, space, dimension, consciousness, imagination, deduction, intuition, sensation, and sensory perception. In order to grasp the nature of the world, we must seek for points of comparison between these different modes of investigation, a common denominator for things that appear at first to belong to different orders. The various modes of knowledge must thus be integrated into an overall concept.

The only form of expression common to all the various notions of the nature of the world, or rather of appearance, is probably energetic and mathematical. This does not mean, however, that number, or more precisely the "computable" (*gana*), can itself be considered the fundamental aspect of all manifestations. Rather, it is a form of language that can be used to analyze, express, and connect the various levels of cosmic or apparent reality. The god Ganapati[1] symbolizes the preeminence of the computable. Between the nature of the world and the symbols of mathematical language there exist the same difference and the same interdependence as between man's thoughts and the symbols of the spoken word. Mathematical language seems to be the form of expression closest to the one used by the Cosmic Being to express its thought in Creation.

The various elements constituting what is called matter can be reduced to a few ratios between the basic energetic components. This is the theory of *Maya,* or Creative Illusion, which reduces all substance, all thought, and all life to forms of energy (more or less complex groupings of forces or oriented tendencies) in a substratum that can be called Time (*Kala*), Space (*Akasha*), the Universal Soul (*Atman*), or the Conscious Immensity (*Brahman*), according to the envisaged aspect of the world.

An observation of the workings of our brain leads to a similar concept. The expression of thought can be reduced to a play of combinations, forces, tendencies, and currents, offering a considerable, if limited, number of possibilities. Furthermore, this explains why, to a certain extent, thought is expressed by a group of symbols—words—which are kept in a dictionary and which can themselves be reduced to a very limited number of roots, taking up only a few pages. We do not feel, however, that our thought is made inert because it is circumscribed by the restraints of a fixed vocabulary. The play of language, which moves words like the colored glass of a kaleidoscope, probably corresponds quite well to the play of currents forming cosmic thought, which is the substance of creation and is the basis of the concept of the Creative Word.

Sensation links thought to the outside world and is essentially

---

1. A. Daniélou, *The Myths and Gods of India* (Rochester, Vt.: Inner Traditions International, 1991), pp. 291–297.

a perception of relations, which can be expressed in often extremely precise numerical forms that relate to sounds, colors, temperature, shape, and so on. The substrata of space and duration can be expressed only in mathematical terms. Life is but a dimension added to matter, which links it to sensation, which in turn appears to be linked to characteristics that can be expressed by numerical formulas.

If all the aspects of existence are studied from the common standpoint of mathematical relations, simple factors are discovered in every case, which seem to play an essential role. At this point, numerology becomes a fundamental instrument of science. For example, certain aspects of existence are inevitably found in pairs, others in threes, fours, fives, sevens, elevens, twelves, and one hundred and eights. The fact of finding one or more of these factors in any aspect of life, existence, man, or society indicates a certain relationship with other apparently unrelated phenomena and may thus be a key to the integration of the various orders of existence, which will then appear as the expression or symbols of a transcendent and divine order.

Numerology can be used to classify minerals,[2] vegetables, and men, establishing relationships between them according to categories expressing a fundamental order of being and corresponding to the profound, inexorable nature of Creation. In studying the elements constituting inert or living matter, cells, or molecules, characteristics of a numerical order are found at all levels of any substance or being, just as the forms of a crystal reveal the structure of its molecules.

CREATION AND PERCEPTION

When an eddy appears in the immobile and neutral substratum of Universal Consciousness, a tendency is polarized. This tendency is

---

2. Modern physics differentiates elements, atoms, and molecules according to numerical differences, in terms of force ratio.

composed of insubstantial energy and manifests itself as an intention, or oriented tension. According to the Upanishads, the first notion formed in the latent awakening consciousness is fear, the most rudimentary of feelings. Fear gives birth to all the other feelings, are but palliatives or diversions masking basic fear, the source of all consciousness. The fear of separation from the fundamental Unity of Creation is always found at the root of all action, all belief, all religion, all knowledge—not only on the human plane, where it can be easily observed, but at all levels of creation, whether animated, living or inert, conscious or unconscious.

> By fear of him the Sun shines, and the wind and fire perform their tasks.   (Chandogya Upanishad)

From this elemental fear is born Cosmic Consciousness: the desire to think, create, and produce something outside itself, to last and not merely to be in an eternally unformed neutral state. When it appears in the Cosmic Consciousness, the resulting thought gives birth to the Universe; rather, the Universe is not distinct from the thought. The desire to create, the source of all cosmic thought, produced by the vibration born of the first tension in the cosmic substratum, is itself the Universe and what we perceive as the apparent reality of the world.

It is at this point that the role of the microcosms appears: living beings that are miniature antiuniverses, tiny thinking and conscious cosmoses. They are, however, inverted; their very perception gives the Universe a dimension, an appearance of reality, giving cosmic thought the illusion of material reality. Standing at the top of the ladder of living beings in the sector of the perceived Universe, man plays an essential role in the play of creative thought, which thus ceases to be a dream because it is perceived from without.

Man thus envisaged finds his reason for being. The very limits of his perceptions give the Universe the form that his senses transmit to his consciousness. The divine dream takes on an independent shape, determined by the limits in the perceptions of the witness, through whom, and through the illusion of independent centers of existence, the Cosmic Consciousness can finally see its dream projected outside itself. The Universe exists in man for the Cosmic Being, as it exists in the Cosmic Being for man. It is by means of and through this dualism that the Universal Consciousness is made manifest. This is the meaning of the myth of Narcissus.

The reality of a particular Universe thus resides solely in the limits given it by the perception of conscious individuals, whose consciousness is in appearance, but only in appearance, separate from the Universal Consciousness. The role of gods, spirits, and the various species of men and animals is that of receivers, which, through the various limitations of their perception, provide different facets to the cosmic dream, whose reality becomes one, yet multiple. They are vital counterparts to the omniscient Cosmic Being, who is conscious of the dream's unreality in the play of creation and therefore needs to fashion individuals with a limited consciousness to provide the illusion of its own reality.

Like the Universe to which they give reality, beings exist only in proportion to their own imperfection. No being could exist that could simultaneously exist and be without limitations. An angel, or a God, if he exists, cannot be omniscient.

Whatever the duration and extent of microcosmic consciousness, whatever the final destiny of the human being—immortal or perishable (inevitably both, but on different levels)—his role as witness explains his nature and justifies his existence, as is evidenced in all aspects of his life and collective and individual development.

The physical or moral laws to which man is subject, and according to which he functions collectively and individually, either are applications of the reflections of cosmic laws, necessarily formulated before his appearance in the Creator's mind, or are otherwise merely more or less absurd, arbitrary, and useless conventions. The body of laws by which the world was created inevitably existed prior to its birth. It would be impossible to invent a spatial world without first creating the laws of space, or a world of atoms without there first existing a principle of forces governing their cohesion and organization, or yet a human world in which the values defining man's role do not precede the physical appearance of mankind.

The attraction of opposites, space, movement, orientation, time, gravity, and all the laws that govern the spheres and the potentiality of life must necessarily be defined before either the spheres or life itself can appear. This natural law forms the substratum of the creative thought of the Cosmic Being and is called dharma, the world's moral nature or law. All things must conform to it in order to realize their destiny, aim, and usefulness.

The scope of all knowledge and all science is to discover these laws governing the inner nature of things and regulating their development. Any speculation that does not take these laws into account is an arbitrary, imaginary creation, an abstraction corresponding to a world that may be possible but is not the world in which we live. The laws that govern thought mechanisms and the vital functions of living beings are of the same nature as those governing the forms, proportions, and numerical and geometrical properties of the world of the stars as well as inanimate matter. Being at a rather more complex level, the basic structures of life are merely less apparent.

The general name *Veda*—a word meaning "vision" and, as a corollary, "object of knowledge"—is given by the Hindus to the body of laws governing the Universe before and since its appearance, since perception of these natural laws is the object of all knowledge, science, and learning. The texts known as Vedas are merely the revelation or codification of certain aspects of that body of eternal laws that exist of themselves beyond all manifestation, all revelation, and all perception—the basis of the system on which the world was created. The Vedas are considered hermetic, symbolic texts, which reveal their meaning only to those who possess the key. Their purpose is merely to guide man in the domains necessary for orienting his life. The Vedas are but a fragment of the universal Veda.

By study and research in these immutable and fundamental laws that explain man's nature and role, Hindu philosophy envisages the possibility of defining certain principles as the basis for the rules of human life and of establishing a scheme for a stable society that gives each human being the possibility of realizing to the full his role and destiny. To the extent to which he reaches this aim, man can cooperate in the Creator's work and find his personal and social equilibrium and happiness.

At this point, man may exceed his passive role as witness, realizing a spiritual destiny by means of which he can escape human limitations and the cycle of life and death and can unite with the divine, returning to the state of potentiality from which he came forth. Metaphysics, psychology, and sociology are precise sciences for Hindus, like physics and mathematics, since like all sciences they lead to a search for laws that exist of themselves, beyond all subjectivity. All modern social theories that are inspired by imaginary ideals in the absence of a search to understand man's individual and social nature and his role in the divine plan, and that seek to deny the factual differences existing in the hierarchy of nature as well as the technically different roles for which the various types of mankind are predestined and were specifically created, appear aberrant and antiscientific from the Hindu point of view, leading only to social disorder and the frustration of the individual, society and race. It is evident that if man does not fulfil his role, the Creator has no reason for not suppressing him. According to the Hindus, this has already happened several times in the world's long history, our human predecessors having been replaced with a species better adapted and more aware of its function.

Modern societies seem to ignore the role played by mankind as a whole, apparently formed of individuals but with a collective role in creation. They also ignore the hierarchy of species and tend to reject mutations and exceptional beings.

MATTER, THE STARS, AND LIFE

In Hindu thought there is no irreducible dualism, or real opposition in the play of opposites that constitutes the field of our perceptions. Whether spirit and matter, consciousness and unconsciousness, inert and living, day and night, white and black, good and evil, or active and passive, it is merely a question of opposition between complementary and interdependent elements, which exist only in relation to each other.

The Universe is a speculation, a play of probabilities and possibilities, which is not unique and which could be different in other dimensions or other space. Modern science is discovering a little more every day about such possibilities. The Cosmic Being ceaselessly invents other universes existing on planes other than the one we perceive. These mental fantasies of the Cosmic Being are universes that are imagined but not materialized, which Hindu symbolism presents as the Apsaras, heavenly nymphs, noncreated potentialities. Even within the world we believe we know, there are other worlds with different orders of dimension and perception, giving rise to different realities. Although separate at certain levels, they interconnect at others. Even on the plane of what is perceptible to us, there is no division between the various levels of creation or between matter, life, thought, and consciousness. There are merely differences of dimension, modality, moment, or degree. Matter is not unconscious, but on our scale of perception it has no organ to assume individuality or coordinate its diffuse receptivity, as is the case with the individual cells of the body. Matter appears to be subject to the laws of space and time, but on the scale of our perception, it has no instrument for measuring, appreciating, or being conscious of them and thus has no dimension. Nothing leads us to surmise that the same occurs on the scale of the atom or of the planetary system and that the possibility of solar consciousness as envisaged by Hindu cosmology does not exist. Since the earth came forth from the sun, nothing on earth can exist—neither life, thought, nor consciousness—that does not belong to its solar nature.

In traditional Hindu teaching, astronomy and astrology are not considered to be separate sciences. According to the classical treatises still used in the colleges of astrology at Indian universities, the planets represent degrees of consciousness on an astronomical scale—various tendencies punctuating the evolution of the terrestrial world. The sun, from which our little world came forth, represents the sum of everything that we are. Thus there exist solar consciousness, solar thought, solar memory, solar matter, and solar intelligence: whence otherwise came these different elements into our world, which is a mere splinter of the sun itself? We have no way of knowing whether the currents that move in our brain, which we call thought, could not seem to a microscopic observer like the movements that agitate the sun's surface.

Stars appear to have no power of independent action, and all their movements seem predictable and interchangeable. This is only true, however, from our own point of view and scale of measurement; the cells of our body could also be considered automatons in this fashion. Existing in oriented time, we are unable to grasp the nature of anything in our world that evolves in reversible time or that has values other than duration, or for whom a millennium of our time is but an instant, which can be conceived as space vehicles existing in a different time duration and remaining motionless for a long period, becoming perceptible to us only for an instant.

It is the same at the level of atoms, whose structure is very similar to that of the solar system, but which operate in different dimensions of time and space. The space inside an atom is different from the space we know; one cannot be measured in terms of the other. In itself, an atom is as vast as a galaxy. There is no limit to the possibility of worlds contained one within another. Even at the level of human perception, there exists an infinity of stellar and planetary worlds comparable to our own, with living beings who may resemble us in many ways. The earth and man are not unique, isolated phenomena.

Long before modern scholars, the Hindus observed that the first stage of consciousness, or life, appears to human perception in the phenomenon of crystallization. Crystals reveal the numerical nature of their substance and represent a first step toward the living and conscious organism. Then come vegetable forms and lower animals, which, almost imperceptibly at first, orient themselves in different directions. Climbing plants demonstrate a more consciously organized degree of vegetable life than do other plants.

Observations on the sensitivity, subjectivity, and emotive receptivity of plants have always interested the Hindus. The recent works of the famous Hindu scholar Jagadish Chandra Bose have established elements of subjectivity, sympathy, emotion, joy, and suffering among plants, which have been the subject of important publications.

The forms of animal life present varying degrees of consciousness. Animals have much more complex sensory organs than plants, at times even more complex than our own. They move in a time dimension very close to ours. In each order of life, whether animal, vegetable, or mineral, a hierarchy can be established according to the predominance of the three fundamental tendencies, which are the very basis of all existence, all appearance, and all life. These fundamental tendencies are *sattva,* the tendency to cohesion and light, *tamas,* the tendency to disintegration and darkness, and *rajas,* the tendency to revolution, activity, and movement.

Like man's nature, that of plants, minerals, and animals can be determined by the variable and complex relation established by the proportion of the three tendencies in each component element. Forms of life can thus be oriented differently, and according to our own nature and the aims we pursue, contact with them can be beneficial or maleficent. Therefore, a sacred character is attributed to certain plants or animals.

Naturally, these three tendencies are present in the structure of every human being and every object. They cannot exist without each other, but the relative predominance of one or the other determines the quality, orientation, and destiny of any species or individual. The predominance of certain tendencies also characterizes the various human races and should guide their relations with one another.

4 THE FOUR AIMS OF LIFE

THE FOUR "AIMS OF LIFE" (PURUSHARTHAS)

The life of a man (*purusha*) has four aims or meanings (*artha*) and is not complete until all four have been accomplished. If any one of the four is ignored, accomplishment is not possible. The four aims are these:

Dharma—duty, virtue, man's striving to perfect what he is: self-realization on the moral level (courage, honesty, tolerance, charity)

Artha—"means," wealth, success, family, the acquisition of material goods: self-realization on the social or active level

Kama—pleasure, sexuality, enjoyment in all its forms: self-realization on the sensual level

Moksha—final and total liberation from the chains of existence: self-realization on the spiritual level

Man must keep these four aims in mind in all his actions and at all moments of his life. If he neglects one he is certain to fail in the others. The first three aims of life determine the value of the human being:

> *As honey is the essence of the flower, pleasure is the accomplishment of desire. Virtue, wealth, and pleasure must all be sought together. He who only seeks one of the three is unworthy; he who seeks but two is mediocre. The best is he who seeks all three.* (Mahabharata)

A man who ignores the duties of rank, caste, and profession, which according to the Hindus' integrated concept of life are aspects of his nature, and who does not fulfil his inner and outer self, destroys the material conditions that allow him to attain spiritual fulfilment and to pay his debts to the gods, his ancestors, and the sages. In the *Bhagavad Gita,* when the prince-soldier Arjuna wishes to abjure a fratricidal war and refuses to take part in the massacre of his brothers-in-law, cousins, and uncles and speaks of withdrawing to a contemplative life in order to devote himself to the quest of the divine, the god Krishna, who guides his chariot, harshly reminds him of his duties and warrior virtues and warns him against a renunciation that would only be failure, the neglect of his duty as a soldier, and the overlooking of his own nature.

Those who are indifferent to work, to a profession, to riches and power and who do not seek to acquire them are incapable of fulfilling their destiny because the other three aims of life require material tranquility and standing in society, since man has a collective as well as an individual nature. The vagabond or the poor man cannot accomplish his social duty, is deprived of sensual pleasures, and does not possess the inner calm and physical balance that would allow him to devote himself to his own interior progress once he has discharged his material and moral debts.

Our body is the instrument of our destiny. Our intellectual mechanism and spiritual being are not independent of the body that shelters and nourishes them. If we wish for success in anything whatever, we must take care of our body: cherish, satisfy, and content it. Yogis condemn abstinence, just as they condemn excess, since both cause imbalance in the physical and intellectual being. A healthy, vigorous, satisfied body, one that is pleasant to inhabit, is the best vehicle and instrument for human and spiritual accomplishment. Eroticism and pleasure in all its forms are vital for man's intellectual and physical balance. Life is transmitted through the sexual act, and the giving of life is a duty, a debt to be discharged by whoever has received it. Besides its practical utility, however, physical pleasure plays an essential role in our inner development. It is the image of divine bliss and prepares us and aids us to attain it. A man who strives to be chaste and who fears, condemns, and thwarts physical love can never free himself from the prison of the senses. He weaves around himself a web of obscure frustrations, which will hinder him from realizing his transcendental destiny.

On the other hand, the man who has tasted all kinds of sensual pleasure can gradually turn aside from them, finding greater sensual pleasure in union with the divine. This is no longer renunciation, but liberation. In discovering the divine, the realized man gradually loses interest in earthly things, virtue, honor, vice, and pleasure. He does not fear the sight of virtue or the spectacle of the sensual pleasures of others. He considers the human act of love in the same way that he breathes the perfume of flowers or listens to the song of the birds, conscious of the harmony of the divine illusion that is the world, to which only the reality of the divine can be preferred, perceived in the silence of nonthinking and nonacting.

The remark of the saint who said "I have never renounced any vice: it is they that have left me" summarizes the Hindu attitude to pleasure.

To cooperate in others' pleasures is also a duty. "Never repulse a woman who offers herself," says the *Chandogya Upanishad.*

Only after fulfilment of the other aims of life can the final goal be attained—total detachment leading man to liberation (moksha), the fourth and veritable meaning of human life.

Because they forget that spiritual realization is the real and final aim of life, men chain themselves to ambitions that do not accord with their true nature, thus creating social disorder. A good shoemaker is essential to society and in practicing his art can fulfil the four aims of life. This does not mean, however, that he necessarily possesses the aptitudes and moral virtues needed to make him a political leader, a head of state, a philosopher, or a prostitute.

External accomplishment reflects the inner being. There is a fundamental relationship between external and inner fulfilment, the two forms of expression of the same being. This is why the possession of material goods is connected with the sense of duty, with the virtues of order and conformity that correspond to the cohesive, constructive, and cumulative tendency (sattva), whereas the search for physical pleasure is connected with the search for divine bliss, since both issue from the dissolving or destructive tendency (tamas). Wealth is a reflection of virtue, whereas the union of two bodies reflects union with the divine. The aims of life are thus always envisaged in pairs, according to a given order: Dharma and Artha in the center and Kama and Moksha on either side—duties and material goods on one side, and pleasure and liberation on the other. Being furthest from liberation, duty and virtue are the greatest obstacles to its accomplishment. It is the renunciation of virtues, not vices, which are unimportant, that the Bhagavad Gita recommends to the seeker after God.

The three tendencies and the four aims of life are related thus:

Moksha = Tamas (dispersion)
Dharma = Sattva (cohesion)
Rajas (activity)
Artha = Sattva (cohesion)
Kama = Tamas (dispersion)

Action (Karma)

Our actions play a fundamental role in the realization of our human and spiritual destiny. Until we attain the state of constant contemplation in nonaction, and as long as the greater part of our

70

life consists of actions, the value of the latter affects our nature and gradually transforms us.

According to the theory of action, or *karma,* our being is the result of our past actions. During our life, a certain number of positive actions make us different from the person we were when we were born, thus determining a better or worse destiny in our future lives until final liberation is reached. At this moment, the incarnate being, made perfect by his actions, liberates himself and, renouncing all virtues and all vices, plunges into the ocean of nonaction, submerging into the absolute being, or nonbeing, according to how the ultimate substratum of the cosmic universe is regarded.

Each species of being is governed by a natural law, an ethical nature that determines the value of every action. Every individual must fulfil his role in the harmony of creation, which involves conforming to his moral nature, the dharmas of his species, race, caste, and person, and can be considered the negative side of ethics. Only then, once his obligations have been fulfilled, may man by his behavior improve his nature through positive action and approach liberation, or fusion with the impersonal, the Cosmic Being. He will thus cease to exist as a simple link in the chain of his species by bringing to fruition the efforts made by his ancestors for reintegration with the divine being.

As a man acts, as he behaves, so he becomes.
He who performs good actions, becomes good.
He who commits crime becomes a criminal.
By virtuous actions, a man becomes virtuous.
By evil actions, evil.
It is said that man becomes what he desires.
His will follows his desire, as his actions his will.
He becomes conform to his actions.

He that desires what he desires with all his heart is reborn
with what he desires in the very place he desired it.
(Brihadaranyaka Upanishad, 4.4.5)

71

Evil actions performed in this world do not bear fruit immediately like the cow, which gives milk after being fed, but gradually gnaw the roots of him who commits them.   *(Manu, 4.172)*

Birth is not governed by chance. The fact of being born intelligent, strong, handsome, and rich, while another is born stupid, ugly, and sickly, is not just a matter of chance or the whim of an unjust and irresponsible creator nor is whether one is born as a man, an angel, or an animal.

The inequalities and cruelty of the world cannot be ascribed to God. Not without reason did God make creatures unequal, but what is the reason? We believe it is the result of man's accomplishing or neglecting his duties.
                                        (Brahma-sutra bhashya, 2.1.34)

At birth, every individual starts out at a certain level of development, ranging from the unconscious to the conscious, from the inanimate to the transcendent, from innocence to spiritual maturity. The individual is the result of his actions in previous lives, the fruit of a long chain of actions. It matters little whether our former lives demonstrate the continuity of the transmigrating ego from one unrelated body to another, or else a succession of ancestral egos perpetuated in the same flesh in bodies connected by heredity. The nature of the ego, considered a disincarnate and transmigrating memory that alone could establish a link between physically unconnected bodies, is a problem that man, centered on the vanity of an illusory self, prefers not to approach.

From a certain point of view, the possibility that memory elements are inherited along with other characteristics seems more likely than that a disincarnate self always refinds itself in ephemeral bodies that it changes as one changes a car. The connections between the physical brain, memory, and mind appear far too close for the second hypothesis to be taken very seriously.

In any event, regardless of individual or collective causes, an infant is born with an active and a passive element that explain his nature and justify what he is at birth and that give him a precise place in the hierarchy of creation and thus a certain role to fulfil. It is by fulfilling and transcending this role, in surpassing but not ignoring his nature and function, that he can progress toward more developed states and toward final liberation. Man liberates himself gradually from the collective life of his species, race, and caste and tends toward an autonomous individuality. Then, and only then, on attaining real individuality, can he liberate himself, reintegrating with the causal substratum and ceasing to exist as an individual and transmigrant being.

First of all, therefore, man is a link in the endless chain of humanity. He is the result of the characteristics accumulated by his ancestors. He himself must perfect the link he represents in order to pass it on to the next, and this is why, to the Hindu, he must observe all the rules that assure the continuation of his type, his race, of what he received as a gift at birth. If he brings this development to a stop by attaining perfection and liberation, he fulfils the efforts of his ancestors, but if he breaks the chain by procreating a child of mixed race or caste, he burdens himself with a debt he can never repay and draws upon himself and his descendants the curse of the gods and his ancestors.

The idea of metempsychosis, originating in Jain philosophy, gives an exaggerated importance to the individual as though he were an isolated phenomenon, instead of envisaging the collective aspect of humanity as a whole and giving preference to a transmigrant rather than a transmitted ego.

5 THE FIRST AIM OF LIFE

DHARMA: DUTY, VIRTUE

Self-realization on the Moral Plane

ETHICS

The fulfilment of duty, the realization by each being of that for which he was created, is the very basis of existence. He who accomplishes his duty is respected by all. Duty fulfilled obliterates evil. Everything is based on the fulfilling of duty. This is why it is said that the most important thing is duty. (Taittiriya Aranyaka, 10.63)

It is difficult to explain Hindu moral attitudes using a Western vocabulary fashioned by Christian scholasticism; it is not even easy to establish parallels between terms, postulates, and classifications. The very values are so contradictory that in passing from one of these worlds to the other, it is necessary to think on another plane and in another idiom, without being able to coordinate the two, and to react normally at either level without taking into account the reactions that would have occurred on the other plane. Such a situation may involve opposing indignantly on one side what one approves on the other,

74

virtuously avoiding certain actions on the one level that have not the slightest importance on the other. Most of the values we take for ethics are merely ritualized conventions, forms of politeness, or good manners. A respectable person avoids committing certain acts and saying certain things, but unfortunately such acts and words vary greatly from one civilization to another.

For Hindus, ethics does not involve applying a code of laws dictated by men, prophets, or gods. Moral law, like physical law, existed before the world began and expresses the nature of things and beings. These constants govern our conduct; they are the rules that are necessary to make the stars and planets work, the laws that atoms, vegetables, and human and animal societies all obey. The aim of all science and all knowledge is to grasp a few fragments of these fundamental and universal laws.

Man's social nature is not his only side; it reflects but one aspect of his being, which may not even be the most important. Man's first duty to himself is to seek to analyze and understand his own nature and to find the means of self-realization, which may well be contrary to his collective nature and his social duty. Above all else, man's responsibility is toward himself, avoiding the involvement of others and, as far as possible, any conflict between his individual and his social nature.

The natural, fundamental laws that govern human society and the development of the individual can be discovered only by difficult and subtle research. They exist of and by themselves. Man was created in accordance with these laws and must know them in order to understand himself and evaluate his actions. In the Hindu view, if we seek to build a society against nature—a society without castes, for example—we are certain to destroy ourselves, since such a society can never work efficiently and does not conform to the divine plan. It is like trying to build a house without taking into account the laws of gravity. Ethics is thus, first of all, a science—a form of research. It is not a revealed dogma or a majority resolution, but a study of the rules of conduct that are natural to man and take account of the different aspects of his physical, psychic, transmigrant, and spiritual nature, as well as his collective functions, role, destiny, and purpose in the cosmic order. Like all science, ethics must remain open to new discoveries and to changes in the conditions of life caused by the great passage of cycles.

Ethics cannot therefore be fixed by immutable laws or by edict. Similarly, Hindu law, which differs for each caste and each racial or professional grouping, has also varied from one period to another within each group. Adaptations are suggested by a sort of group council when a basic principle of social rights, concerning the government of the state, is affected.

All admit that unrestricted personal liberty is impossible: society could not exist if the individual were free to kill, rape, steal, or simply meddle in others' business instead of attending to his own. When an individual does not conform to laws that restrict certain aspects of freedom in order to protect others, society arrogates the right to take away his freedom and imprison him or even to put him to death. By extending the idea of curtailing certain liberties so as to protect others to the ethnic group instead of limiting it to the individual, the ethic of caste is obtained. The Tenth Commandment in the Hebrew Bible says, "Thou shalt not covet thy neighbor's wife, nor anything that is thy neighbor's," whereas the caste ethic says, "Thou shalt not take a wife from the neighboring group, nor its means of livelihood."

Just as the law that prevents our neighbor from taking our wife guarantees that we can live in harmony with him, without fear and without defenses, the severe laws forbidding the mixing of the castes allow the most varied races, civilizations, and religions to exist side by side without fear or conflict.

> *Moral law is defined so that man will not injure his neighbor. Moral law is certain to be found wherever human beings refrain from mutual harm.* (Mahabharata)

There are three kinds of rules of behavior: general rules, group or caste rules, and individual rules. Social ethics are common to all three and comprise the elementary conventions required for the smooth running of society. However, these rules are usually of a practical order, must be as limited as possible, and must not interfere in private life or caste affairs. The state is not competent to regulate sexual habits, marriage and divorce, or inheritance, whose rules vary according to caste and religion. Nor should it regulate the use of alcohol and other drugs, which are forbidden to Brahmans and merchants but permitted to the other castes.

Only too easily do we accept that our armies pillage and kill "the enemy," whoever he may be, whether the inhabitants of the next village or of a neighboring country, or simply men belonging to another religion, as though the wearing of a uniform or the pretext of national necessity could change the nature of the act. General rules of behavior are unavoidably amoral. Social ethics thus appear as a purely human convention, confined to the elementary rules of coexistence, and should not be attributed any value as far as man's spiritual destiny is concerned.

> *The ten elements of common moral duty are courage, tolerance, humility, honesty, cleanliness, self-control, understanding, knowledge, truth, and calm.*
>
> (Manu, 6.92)

> *Not to get angry, to tell the truth, share one's possessions, forgive, be compassionate, give children to one's wife, not to nurture grievances, to be honest, to feed one's dependents, are the nine virtues which must be practised by all.* (Mahabharata)

Group or caste ethic is based on the different origins, nature, and functions of each social group and its different duties—the virtues of the Brahman or the soldier, the merchant or the craftsman, the man or the woman—which assure the survival and independence of each group and its inclusion in society as a whole. The Hindu lawgivers sought to understand and codify the rules of conduct for the different groups and castes, at all levels. Most of these rules are on the social plane and serve to establish the stability of society and to distribute its privileges equably.

Each individual is subject to a hierarchy of duties.

First come the duties of caste, then the duties relative to each age of life, then the duties combining caste and age, and finally, those due to special circumstances.

(Hemadri)

Given the differences of function and aptitude of the various human beings, the duties and rules of conduct for each are also different. The duties of man and woman are often contradictory. The servant's virtues differ from those of his master. A king's duties and rules of conduct are not the same as for his ministers or subjects.

The first duties are easy to fulfil. They consist of conforming to the rules of one's social milieu, caste, and corporation, which in a well-organized society should not hamper the individual's freedom to develop and realize himself fully. The dharma of the Brahman is different from that of the soldier, the merchant, or the craftsman. For example, priests and merchants are usually vegetarians, which is not required of soldiers or craftsmen. It is no virtue for a soldier to be vegetarian; that would harm his functional metabolism. Similarly, it is a serious fault for a scholar to touch dead flesh, because meat, which stimulates physical activity, is prejudicial to the inner calm of the thinker.

Brahmans

A priest may possess only very few belongings, while the merchant must accumulate riches so that he can give work to the workman and support the temples and scholars with his gifts. A prince must practice the arts of hunting and war, and the craftsman his family profession, while the scholar must dedicate himself to his studies. By fulfilling his own role, each reaches perfection in his being and estate. The ignorant priest, the weak or cowardly prince, the lazy worker or free-spending merchant, for whatever cause or reason, are not fulfilling their role. They are neither decorative nor useful, since they neglect their social function and disturb the order and harmony of the nation, nor is it likely that they can fulfil the duties of another social group. A merchant can no more be made into a knight than a lion can be made from a sheep.

The duties of Brahmans, Kshatriyas, Vaishyas, and Shudras are assigned to them according to the qualities inherent in their natures. (Bhagavad Gita, 18.41-42)

Selflessness and study are the virtues of Brahmans.

An even temper, self-control, austerity, cleanliness, forgiveness, honesty, duty, wisdom, and faith are the duties that are compatible with the Brahman's nature.
(Bhagavad Gita, 18.42)

A Brahman must be monogamous, although he is allowed a second wife if the first is sterile. This rule, however, does not exclude his right to visit prostitutes; as already stated, pleasure is something different from, and independent of, marriage and the family. A Brahman must, however, observe strict rules of purification, bathing three times a day and avoiding all contact with objects or persons deemed polluted. He has to dedicate himself to study and teaching, and his possessions are extremely limited. He may not partake of meat, alcohol, or in some cases those parts of a plant growing below ground (onions, garlic, potatoes). He must also perform the rites and three daily meditations (*sandhya*). In return for his asceticism, he is honored and respected by all and is thereby paid for his efforts. At this point, we are still on the level of human values, which although creating a favorable atmosphere for spiritual progress, have no other connections with it. A poor Brahman may have to accept a neutral job—as a liftboy, for example—but the rich merchant who employs him will treat him with the greatest respect. Questions of relative wealth have absolutely nothing to do with social rank.

Kshatriyas

The virtues of a prince are courage and justice.

Courage, aggressiveness, endurance, dexterity, never fleeing the battle, generosity, the taste for power, are the duties compatible with the nature of the Kshatriyas.
(Bhagavad Gita, 18.43)

The warrior, whether prince or soldier, is entitled to many wives and good living. He must risk his life to defend his country and must study the arts of war and assure justice for all. Hindu kings have been known to commit suicide because a miscarriage of justice occurred in their dominions (see *Shilappadikaram* for an example of this kind[1]).

Vaishyas

Honesty and charity are the virtues of farmers and merchants.

Agriculture, cattle-breeding and trade are the Vaishyas' duties and compatible with their nature.
(Bhagavad Gita, *18.43*)

The rules of life of the farmer and the merchant resemble those of the Brahman, but instead of study and teaching, their duty is toward agriculture, business, and the economic life of the country, whose prosperity is essential to the proper functioning of society, the state, and religious rites. They must live comfortably but without ostentation, contributing the necessary funds to monasteries, temples, and cultural and charitable institutions.

Shudras

Patience, manual skill, and love of his work are the virtues of the craftsman.

Serving others is the Shudra's duty and is compatible with his nature. (Bhagavad Gita, *18.44*)

The Shudra's life has the greatest freedom. His duty consists of loving his work, respecting the other castes, and serving them

---

1. Ilango Adigal, *The Ankle Bracelet (Shilappadikaram)*, translated from the Tamil by Alain Daniélou (New York: New Directions, 1965).

faithfully and honestly. Furthermore, he can practice polygamy and divorce, can eat whatever he likes, get drunk, and amuse himself as he pleases. His actions have very few social consequences, and from many points of view he is the most unrestricted and freest of the Hindus. He prides himself on his condition and rarely envies the fortunes and duties of other castes. Since most professions are artisanal, the Shudras or their equivalents form by far the most numerous group among the population in all countries and civilizations.

The division of duties and privileges corresponds to what might be termed a theory of equivalents, as opposed to the theory of equality. For the Hindu, men are basically unequal and different, but in order to make the best of this inequality and to prevent it from becoming a social injustice, each must be given different privileges. This can be done only by a society which divides duties and privileges equitably among the castes, as it also does for the individual, the periods of whose life are divided into childhood, adolescence, maturity, and old age.

The forms of duty arising from special circumstances include women's duties, the duties of all in the event of a cataclysm or public distress, and many others. In the *Mahabharata*, Bhisma explains to King Yudhishthira, "I speak only of the most general duties. There is no end as far as special duties are concerned" (*Mahabharata, Shanti parva*, 7.1.2).

Societies in which power is derived from money, as in the Western capitalist world, or where money is derived from power, as in the so-called socialist countries, are fundamentally unjust.

Caste has nothing to do with economic condition. Many poor Brahmans perform menial tasks and are employed by Shudra millionaires but maintain their prorogatives nonetheless. In cases of necessity, a Brahman may take on paid employment if the job is not contrary to the rules of his caste, but he must not be paid for his functions as priest or scholar. Strictly speaking, a Brahman may work as a porter or watchman but not as a modern salaried university professor, which would involve selling knowledge. Solutions are possible, of course, since a Brahman may receive gifts.

Thus, the porter will read the *Upanishads* in Sanskrit while waiting for someone to ring at the door. His master will speak to him with deference, using his noble scholar's title, and will take care not to defile him by his contact. This conduct all belongs to the realm of normal intercaste relations. The Brahman cook of a rich merchant may not taste the food he prepares, since he may eat nothing in the house of a non-Brahman. At other times, the same man may be the officiating priest at a marriage ceremony or funeral. Performance of a job that we might consider subordinate does not affect his dignity as a Brahman, and no Hindu would understand our social prejudices in this regard. The master's whole family will prostrate themselves before the servant-become-priest without finding it strange or abnormal.

The third order of ethics, that of the individual, is the only true ethic. The others are merely social arrangements that are useful for the development and stability of human society, but they do not affect the inner development of the individual being, which is the essential duty of every person.

It is very difficult to set rules in the domain of personal ethics. Whatever aids the individual in progressing toward the perfecting of what he is, toward his spiritual realization and final liberation, is good, while whatever diverts him or draws him back is bad. In the whole world, however, no two beings are alike: their degree of inner development is different. On the long ladder of life, ascending from unconscious matter to absolute consciousness, we are all on different rungs. All forms of action or conduct corresponding to an earlier stage are clearly a step backward and are therefore bad, whereas for a less developed being the same actions may represent a step forward and are therefore good. A shoemaker may well be closer to sainthood than a proud Brahman. Spiritual progress has nothing to do with social rank. The *Padma Purana* explains that during the Age of Conflicts, the Kali Yuga, in which we are living, women and Shudras have the greater advantage because their duties are easily fulfilled, while it is almost impossible for the princes and priests not to fail in their external obligations and in their dedication to their inner advancement.

Indeed, how can the scholar and the priest do without a salary and hence not sell sacraments and knowledge? How can the knight protect those who place themselves under his protection, when they are wanted by the police? On the other hand, the woman who looks after her husband and children, and the craftsman doing an honest job, are at rights with society and can thus dedicate themselves to their spiritual development. The most enviable status for modern man is that of the worker.

The problem for each individual is therefore to determine his degree of development and his place in the hierarchy of living beings, which can only be performed by difficult introspection. He must then find the way of living, acting, and behaving that provides the proper framework, allowing him to make his inner progress. He must eschew frustrations and psychological entanglements that paralyze his development and prevent him from controlling his discursive thought.

No action, no external or inner attitude is bad in itself. Atheism, debauchery, murder, or prostitution may be, and very often are, stages of liberation that are essential to a particular individual, whereas blind piety, puritanism, and obedience to social convention, which are sources of vanity and pride, are often insurmountable obstacles to inner progress and if imposed on others may completely ruin their chances of human and spiritual perfection and realization.

Individual ethics, man's duty toward himself and toward his spiritual progress which is his true destiny, may easily come into conflict with social or group ethics. Compromises must then be sought. A person may choose to practice a secret life in order to avoid external conflicts, or to limit personal requirements to a tolerable minimum on the social level, or else to withdraw from a particular group, since the individual's spiritual destiny is by far the more important to him.

"Man must sacrifice himself for his family, sacrifice his family for his caste, his caste for his country, his country for the world, and the world for himself," says the Sanskrit proverb.

The concept of individual ethics (which may appear aberrant to others) and the necessity for each man to accomplish his personal and peculiar destiny are fundamental to Hinduism and are experienced by all in one way or another. Hindu society, which is so strict in maintaining its castes, is totally lenient toward individual freedom and the right to be original and nonconformist. While meals may not be shared with family members who do not observe certain rules, they may not be shown any hostility—or more especially, any moral disapproval. Nehru's mother could not share his meals because he had broken his caste laws, but she never reproached him for it. Who may judge the duties and conduct of another? In the Hindu world, no one arrogates to himself such rights, since it implies a criticism of the Creator, who made all beings different from each other. If nonconformity leads a man to commit ritual murder, he is realizing himself on that level at his own risk, but if he is arrested by the police, his judge may in turn consider it his duty to condemn the murderer to death. If that happens, it is part of the game, involving neither passion nor moral condamnation. The man took a risk: he could just have easily broken a leg or been drowned as a result of taking other risks. The judge is an instrument of destiny which only intervenes when strictly necessary, since by overstepping its limits it puts itself in the wrong.

In open, egalitarian, loosely organized societies, conformity, propaganda, and brainwashing appear necessary to make individuals behave coherently. The very rigorousness of Hindu society makes such conformity unnecessary. A social framework that takes into account real human needs on all levels, as well as the very different abilities of the various individuals and ethnic entities, is solid enough to allow nonconformist or exceptional persons the greatest possible freedom. On this plane, for all its strictness, Hindu society appears as a model of tolerance and freedom.

MORAL PURITY, RITUAL PURITY, AND UNTOUCHABILITY

The Hindus' notion of purity is thoroughly realistic. Purity is first a ritual matter governing rules of diet and dress and frequent ablutions. The breaking of dietary rules, even accidentally or involuntarily, is a serious defilement, requiring penitences and purifications that may last weeks to wash it away, even if that is possible. A man who pollutes the well or the food of a Brahman, thus polluting the temple where he officiates and rendering the sacrifice sacrilegious and malevolent, is liable to be punished by death. In orthodox society, a tap of running water in the house would suffice to make a Brahman family outcaste, for who can guarantee the ritual purity of the chemical products employed to purify the water, or of the metals used for the pipes?

A person who prepares food may not wash the floor or remove excrement (whether of an animal or a child) as an elementary measure of hygiene.

Nowadays, such rules are difficult to apply in large cities, and magic formulas serve to change tap water into Ganges water, thereby allowing tolerated, but not encouraged, ritual ablutions.

In Hindu life, a continuous guard is necessary against touch and defilement, a habit that may be difficult to lose in ventures to other civilizations. Despite personal beliefs, this reflex affects even Indian atheists, who occasionally commit minor infractions as a demonstration of their free-thinking liberalism but dare not stray too far from the proprieties.

The Western world's moral obsessions are almost exclusively focused on sex. For Hindus, erotic acts have no importance in themselves as long as they do not lead to an outcaste marriage, which would affect the purity of the race and the family. Christian condemnation of masturbation, sexual relations among children or adolescents, homosexuality, and prostitution appear as absurd to the traditional Hindu as an injunction not to eat apples or to take a nap after lunch. By contrast, the killing of a monkey or the eating of vegetables prepared in a kitchen where a steak has been cooked involve very serious defilement, which could ruin the reputation of an entire family, making it difficult to marry off sons and daughters and placing everyone beyond the pale.

In Hinduism, untouchability is connected with the ritual concept of life. Man's voluntary participation in the universal order, which draws him nearer to the Cosmic Being until he can identify himself in him, requires a constant awareness of the ritual value of every act. All life is ritually organized, nothing being left out—

85

whether eating or defecation, professional or intellectual work, erotic or social acts, all of which involve participating in the natural and cosmic order of things. Any act, if we are aware of its symbolic value, becomes an instrument in the implementation of the divine plan.

There exists, however, an order or hierarchy in our acts, according to the proportion of tamas (the unconscious order), sattva (the conscious order), and rajas (the order of action) they contain. These three elements are the basis of every substance, all being, every action. The differences between human beings are due to their relative proportion. Similarly, a hierarchy can be established for minerals, plants, animals, men, and spirits.

There also exist secret affinities based on particular cellular characteristics, which can be expressed by means of numerological identities between minerals, plants, animals, and men. For example, there is some sort of genetic relation between the species, such as the pippal, the bull, and the Brahman, whence their sacred attributions.

These hierarchies may sometimes be inverted. As is true of Tantric cults, the divine may be sought in the lower infinity, beyond consciousness, in the vile and impure, just as well as in the higher infinity, beyond the conscious, in the noble and pure. In both cases, however, a purification ritual is needed at each step before the next step in the hierarchy of our actions is approached. Ritual purifications thus play a constant and fundamental role in all life's actions. There are various kinds of purification: external purification by means of water, fire, or new or ritually purified clothes; purification of the body by means of breathing exercises and suitable postures; external purification by sacred formulas; and mental purification by means of prayer and methods of concentration.

The body is purified by water, the mind by truth, thought by knowledge and austerity, the intellect by understanding. (Manu, 5.109)

Knowledge, austerity, fire, food, earth, thought, water, ointment, wind, action, sun and time are instruments of purification for living beings. (Manu, 5.105)

Outer cleanliness is preferable to uncleanliness, inner cleanliness to outer cleanliness. But only he that is purified both inwardly and outwardly is truly pure.

(Daksha)

After the natural functions or bodily contact, the ritual bath frees us from defilement, preparing us for the rite of taking food or for entering the sanctuary to perform religious or magical rites. Contact with spilled blood, excrement, men whose occupation is unclean, or animals that eat dead things can cause defilement requiring longer and more complex purifications to restore the state of grace of ritual purity.

All accidental contact with unpurified persons or objects is a defilement, more particularly so for the Brahman, whose ritual impurity risks polluting the temple and in whose case human contacts are strictly controlled. He must avoid touching any man whose rules of purification are less strict than his own, inasmuch as the latter participates only indirectly in the cult of the gods. Brahmans are thus obliged to abstain from physical contact with men of other castes, especially those of certain workers' castes whose occupation requires its members to touch unclean objects, such as leather, meat, garbage, and corpses. Untouchability is therefore an absolute essential for the Brahman's ritual purity, and he must avoid all defilement. Even his wife, during her mentrual periods, is isolated in a pavilion and resumes her domestic functions only after a complete purification of her person, her clothes, and any object she may have touched.

If the shadow of a passerby falls on a Brahman's food, it is thrown to the dogs and another meal must be prepared. If someone from outside the family sets foot in the kitchen, all the food must be thrown away, the utensils must all be cleansed and purified, and the whole kitchen itself replastered with purifying material—generally a mixture of cow dung and mud—before it can be used again.

Since words are sacred for the Brahman, strict silence must be observed during all states of impurity. After sexual congress or a nocturnal emission, the Brahman must bathe in the pure waters of a river or sacred pool before speaking.

Much has been said about untouchables in India, but foreigners' attitudes toward this ritual and social question have singularly shifted the reality of the problem. It is the Brahman who is untouchable, who is incessantly restricted in his acts and his comfort for fear of contacts that would invalidate his sacerdotal duties and his role in society. He is obliged to dig his own well in his garden and not to allow anyone else to draw water from it, simply because he is not allowed to use the public fountains. If a traveler asks a Brahman for water, the latter must draw the water himself and pour it from high above into the waiting receptacle, so as not to touch it.

THE THREE DEBTS OF MAN

Man has three debts to pay. If he desires to free himself from the chains of life, he must first render an account of what he has received and fulfil his obligations, which are three: toward the gods, toward his ancestors, and toward his teachers.

From the gods, man receives the world, the position he occupies, and the whole system to which he belongs, as well as the social order, which is the image of cosmic order governed by divine laws. Man must pay his debt to the gods by worshipping them and nourishing them with the smoke of sacrifices, and by cooperating in the natural order. He must dedicate to the gods the best of himself, as well as the first fruits of the earth and the first grains of rice at each meal. He must sacrifice to them the best kid of the herd and must at all times show them his gratitude for all their gift and protection.

Man must also venerate his ancestors, honor their memory, offer them libations, and above all pay the debt he has contracted by receiving the gift of birth. This debt can only be discharged by begetting a son to continue his line, race, caste, and family. Daughters do not count, since by marriage they pass into another family. Having many children is purely a question of choice or social ambition, to which Hinduism attaches no particular virtue—in fact, rather the opposite. Having nurtured and raised a child and introduced him to life, the parents become the first rank of that child's ancestors. The son must show abundant respect and care for them in their old age, and must especially perform their funeral rites with precision, since it is these rites that free the spirits of the dead from that painful and uncertain state between the death of the physical body and the dissolution of the subtle body.

Man's debt towards the sages, or Rishis, from whom he has received knowledge and the precepts of wisdom, can only be paid by study and by transmitting to others what he has received. The duty of study and teaching, which are the only means of discharging this most onerous of debts, has played a remarkable role in Hindu civilization.

Learned men, sages, monks, and scholars may not retire from the world, despising it and taking no interest therein. They must find disciples who are worthy of receiving and capable of transmitting their burden of learning and must spread the light of their knowledge all around. This is why learned men, wandering monks, and philosophers are met with everywhere, teaching metaphysics or philosophical systems in the village square, or commenting on the sacred texts or the notions of traditional science. This has been highly important in India in giving even the poorest, most humble, and apparently least cultivated a level of philosophical and religious knowledge; a breadth of view; an interest in cosmic, divine, and human laws; and a spirit of tolerance, which is all the more surprising in comparison with the intellectual level of the working classes in countries that consider themselves more technically and economically advanced than India, but where the level of intellectual interest is that of the television.

Only having paid these debts can a man usefully dedicate himself to his own destiny and spiritual realization.

Having studied the holy books, begotten a son, and made sacrifices to the gods according to his means, a man may seek liberation. (Manu, 6.36)

He who does not study the Vedas, does not beget a son, and does not perform the sacrificial rites, will sink into the ocean of form, even while believing that he rises to- wards liberation. (Manu, 6.37)

Man may seek liberation after paying his three debts. He who seeks it without having paid his debts is destined to fail and fall back. (Manu, 6.35)

THE ROLE OF WOMEN

Even more than persons born in different castes, men and women have a very different human and social role. Their very virtues are different, since the consequences of their actions are not the same, and the ethics that govern their conduct are of a different order. The ways leading to their spiritual realization are altogether separate.

There are, indeed, very few common elements in the rules of life for men and women. Furthermore, the social sanctions applied to any serious misdeed are entirely different. Men's relations with prostitutes are inconsequential, while a woman's relations with several men are believed to affect her descendants. Homosexual relations in either case have no importance.

Any attempt to make a common rule of conduct for men and women can only be absurd and harmful to both and to society, since their responsibilities are not the same. Here as elsewhere, the individual has to accept the status and aptitudes that are his by birth and try to perfect himself as he is, not to behave like some- one else. A man who behaves like a woman or a woman who behaves like a man cannot, unless they effectively enter another category, be useful citizens, realize themselves, or find happiness in a future life.

Woman's condition in India and the diversity of her status

90

according to caste or social group reflects the problems of two types of society, the nomadic and the sedentary. The Aryan invasions of the second millennium B.C.E. encountered an essentially sedentary civilization practicing agriculture, trade, and crafts. As is generally the case, this kind of society is matriarchal, a society in which women own, manage, and govern. The woman is the keeper of material goods, which she disposes of and inherits, and her authority is uncontested. The matriarchal system has been maintained by pre-Aryan societies in India to the present day.

The Aryans who invaded India, bringing with them the Vedic religion, were a nomadic pastoral people with a patriarchal type of society. The conflict between the two kinds of society has not yet been resolved. Both forms coexist, although some groups have managed to preserve their original social patterns better than others. The same thing occurred also in Europe, where entirely sedentary populations maintain nomadic, patriarchal institutions, giving rise to a fundamentally irrational form of society. In a sedentary society, under normal circumstances, men live outdoors, making war, hunting, and working far from home, leaving the women responsible for property, house, family, and village organization. Instead of proclaiming the advantages and privileges of the matriarchal system, modern feminist movements often seem to claim, or at least to insert themselves into, those of the patriarchal system without really assuming any of the risks and liabilities. This can in no way lead to a stable, realistic, and constructive situation.

It appears essential, therefore, to attribute to men and women different, complementary roles, as well as distinct privileges and advantages since in no case can their rules of life, ethics, amusements, honors, advantages and taboos, be the same.

For women as for men, a way has to be left open for exceptional beings with special aptitudes. At such a point they automatically enter into another separate category. Female poets, musicians, saints, and those who make pleasure their vocation, are indeed honored, but they belong to sectors that are aesthetically valuable and cease to be links in the chain of the species.

At the level of human society, men's and women's duties are

thus fundamentally irrevocably opposed, and it is only by following their contrary yet complementary laws that the two halves of humanity can fully realize themselves and truly co-operate. From the exoteric point of view, and in those classes taking part in sacerdotal rites, the male principle appears superior. The light, strength, sensuality, and wisdom of man dominate the night, grace, asceticism, and intuition of woman, which is the reason for woman's subjection to man in Hindu thought. The woman is wife, companion, complement, and shadow and realizes herself in this role, in which she is the perfection of herself, attaining by her submission what man must master by force. For his wife, a man can become the very personification of the divine: she needs no other image, and her ritual consists in honoring this god. In worshipping and serving her husband, she fulfils her whole function, the total realization of her physical condition.

Young girls are raised with this idea and without any difficulty consider their husband a sort of god. This is made easier by the fact that the married couple does not live alone but in the family group, in which the women and men are separately organized, and their encounters thus always retain a hint of adventure. Women cannot leave the family kingdom and cannot usually take part in outdoor activities like a man, go hunting, or go to war.

In order to understand woman's position in Hindu society, it must be remembered that the notion of equality of aptitudes, rights, and duties does not exist there at any level. Each human being is born unique, and each category of human beings is unique. In the nearly infinite number of possible combinations of elements making up the human being, it is practically impossible for the same arrangement to be duplicated—for two persons to be absolutely identical, with the same nature, the same appearance, the same function, and the same rank. Human beings can, however, be classified in categories according to their characteristics. In order to realize his own perfection, which is the sole path of inner progress, the individual must determine the class to which he belongs and its relative duties and qualities, as well as the personal characteristics, so as to bring them to bear fruit.

Every man must thus perfect a social and a personal role, which may be profoundly different and even contradictory. The opposition of the two roles is particularly evident in the woman, who is at once humble and exalted, slave and goddess, submissive wife and all-powerful mother.

From an esoteric point of view, the feminine principle is dominant. In secret, magical rites, woman plays an all-important, central role, and the priest worships the goddess and her feminine symbols. Even in the outer world, woman rules over the house—that inner, hidden cell, the sanctuary of which she is the priestess. The father performs his sons' caste initiation rites, but it is the mother whose blessing is required before her son may take the secret path of renunciation, or *sanyasa*.

The esoteric works of the greatest philosopher-poets are dedicated to the glory of the female principle. The highest initiations in monastic orders are in *shakta* form, in which the female aspect of the divinity is worshipped. On the other hand, among the lower castes of a matriarchal character, where the female principle is outwardly predominant, esoterism is phallic. In the secret rites there, the dances, ceremonies, symbols, and invocations emphasize the male aspect of the divine.

In exoteric society—the social order safeguarding the transmission of rites—the higher the rank in the hierarchy, the more important the role of the male, and the more the female role is effaced. The noblest of women, the priest's wife, is the humblest, the most modest, the most untouchable. It is the male, in fact, who is the guardian of the external order, which comprises rites, revealed texts, and inherited knowledge.

At the bottom of the hierarchy, on the other hand, woman prevails over the material order: she reigns and possesses, while the male is a mere impregnator, with a secondary role, lending himself to the arts, pleasures, prayers, and secret rites. For this reason, the family of the priest, or Brahman, is always patriarchal, while the families of the workers' castes are, to differing degrees, matriarchal. In some regions of India, the people—even the kings—are subject to the matriarchal system. Land, house, wealth—all belong to the women, and the daughter inherits from her mother. The men work, play, and make war, whereas the women, sprung from the earth to which they remain close, are the guardians of earth's riches.

In Vedic sacrifices and domestic rituals, the presence and participation of the wife are indispensable. Women have their own sacerdotal role even in public rites and, like men, must prepare for them by fasting and purification.

Like her function in life, woman's nature is dual: all women have two natures, two distinct characters, as both wife and mother. As lover, she represents the strength and creative power of the male principle, which without her is sterile. She is his inspiration, the instrument of his realization, the source of his pleasure. She is the image of Shakti, the power and joy of the gods, who without her would have no existence. It is as mother, however, that woman represents the transcendent aspect of the divine. She is the supreme refuge in which the male plays no role. The goddess mother is the sole source of being, the supreme state of consciousness, the principle of life itself.

Woman is the image of the calm of primordial night for which man yearns, tossed on the waves of life, seeking the state of perfection, the total peace from which he came forth. The universal mother thus appears to man as the supreme state of the divine. The Absolute, Brahma, the indeterminate substratum, is merely an unoriented base. All creation, all thought, all form, all existence come from the mysterious energy that appears in the substratum, this matrix of the great goddess, the universal mother, from whom all forms and beings come.

As mother, woman symbolizes the transcendent aspect of the divine, as mother she is divine and is worshipped. A mother is bereft of artifice. She is man's comfort, wandering through the deserts of the world. She is forgiveness, charity, limitless compassion. The woman who realizes the perfection of her maternal role is the very gate of heaven.

The respect and duty owed to this first of all masters and the authority she retains make the mother an essential and symbolic figure throughout life. The role of mother is a virile role; it has nothing to do with her nature as lover. This is woman's double nature: passive in her relationship with men, active as mother of her children. It is well known, moreover, that the most artificial, most coquettish, and most languid woman, when her child is in danger, becomes courageous and enterprising, heedless of her makeup, her weakness, her hair, or the injuries she might receive. Her nature as mother bears no relation to her nature as lover or seductress. Although her role is basically different from man's, woman is not relegated to an inferior position. She rules over the interior world as man rules over the external world. She is honored, venerated, and always respected.

> *The gods are satisfied wherever women are honored, but where they are not respected, rites and prayers are ineffectual.*
> (Manu, 3.56)

> *Where the wife is happy, the household is happy, but when she is not, nothing is either happy or agreeable.*
> (Manu, 3.62)

Wherever two opposites are found—and according to the cosmic conception of the world, the opposition of active and passive, masculine and feminine is a basic opposition—there are also resultant intermediate states. Sanskrit grammar, which is constructed according to cosmological concepts, has three genders: masculine, feminine, and neuter. It follows inevitably that there are also people who are neither wholly male or wholly female but have parts of both genders and are called *napunsaka* (nonmales). Their duties, social role, and position in society must also be different from those of other human beings.

The neuter category covers many types: eunuchs, physical hermaphrodites, and instinctual or mental hermaphrodites, who may be termed true homosexuals in order to distinguish them from bisexual men who practice homosexuality as a variant in their sexual activities.

Men with androgynous tendencies in whom certain masculine and feminine aspects are united have a special sacred charac-

95

ter, since they symbolize the union of principles, the substance of wealth and of life. Such a man is required to be present during the performance of the sacred mysteries, and his presence is auspicious at important ceremonies, such as weddings. The being in whom masculine and feminine characteristics are united is represented in mythology by Ardha-narishvara, the hermaphroditic aspect of Shiva. There exist extremely secret homosexual rites, associated with the cults of Ganapati and Skanda, the sons of Shiva. Male prostitutes are commonplace in India, where they can be found in almost any village. They live usually as transvestites, forming a separate category or caste with its own religious and social privileges, and play an important role in the arts and in sacred plays organized by the temples. Some years ago, the corporation of male prostitutes officially offered its political support to the Indian government, but the Victorian puritanism rife in modern India prefers to cast a veil over that institution.

According to *Manu* (3.49), a child's sex is the result of the relative vigor of the male and female seed at the moment of conception. If both are of equal strength, either twins will be born or the child will be of intermediate sex.

POPULATION CONTROL

It is vital for Brahmans not to be numerous, so that they form an elite dedicated to sacerdotal functions and remaining over and above the problems of daily life.

Brahmans marry late, only after their studies have been completed, thus sometimes delaying the consummation of marriage, which took place formally during childhood, until they are twenty-five or twenty-six. Like every other action of their life, Brahmans treat the conjugal sexual act as a rite, which is not frequent and takes place only under the appropriate astrological constellation. Brahmans retire early to the third ashrama. Although they may not be celibate like Buddhist monks or Catholic priests, and must marry in order to continue their line, their life has nonetheless a monastic character and requires strong discipline at all levels. Brahmans are encouraged to have small families. Until quite recently, their numbers have been quite limited and have posed no problems of employment beyond their sacerdotal and teaching duties.

Brahmans are strictly monogamous unless their wives are infertile. Extramarital sex is permitted as long as it is childless or (which is the same from the caste point of view) the children cannot claim integration into the priestly caste. Many castes in India, like the scribes in northern India or the Nayars in the South, are the descendents of Brahmans and their mistresses belonging to other castes, outcaste marriage not being legitimate. In the former case, the women were of the merchant caste; in the other, of a non-Aryan warrior caste. A racial mixture automatically creates a new caste, which has no relation with the two castes from which it sprang from the point of view of aptitude, duties, and functions.

For warriors and princes, the problem of overpopulation does not exist. They can thus indulge in widespread polygamy. Wars, accidents, fratricidal struggles, daggers, and poison have always decimated their ranks, and they can never multiply fast enough to keep pace with their losses. Furthermore, polygamy is a practical solution to remedy the loss of so many young men on the battlefield.

The Vaishyas, or merchants, need no particular rule. A rich and propertied class always finds ways to limit its members so as not to scatter its assets.

The demographic problem largely concerns the laboring classes, which are always the most numerous. Their rules of conduct are the least severe, and promiscuity is more widespread, since divorce, repudiation, and even the adultery of married women are without serious consequences and are dealt with by the councils of five notables, elected by the local caste group. Simple means of abortion, usually comprising decoctions of bitter herbs, have been known to Indian medicine for many centuries and have never been considered illegal or immoral. Among the poorer classes, however, and on occasion among all classes, the most efficient means of birth control has always been to expose female children at birth. The perceived advantage of this practice over abortion is the saving of male children and the consequent forming of a numerous working class of constant proportions with a minimum of mouths to feed.

Certain villages in North India could boast ten boys for every one girl when the Europeans first arrived. The prohibition on abandoning female babies and the severe penalties inflicted by English justice have caused an incredible demographic explosion. However, every year many more Indians die of starvation nowadays than there were baby girls that died from exposure one hundred and fifty years ago. Furthermore, the economic conditions and malnutrition of the others has become a tragic endemic problem.

6 THE SECOND AIM OF LIFE

ARTHA: MATERIAL GOODS, WEALTH, SUCCESS, POWER

Self-realization on the Social Level

MATERIAL GOODS

The instrument for any kind of realization is called artha [means]. (Quoted in Siddhanta, p. 183)

The qualities of men and objects are always connected with money. (Shukra niti)

Everything that is an instrument in human realization is called *artha* (means).

Means include education, land, money, cattle, grain, furniture, etc. (Kama Sutra, 1120)

The acquisition of means—material goods, constitutes the most important aim of life; in society, it is on this aim that all the others depend.

*All a king's actions depend on his means, hence on his
treasury.* (Artha Shastra, 2.8)

*For each man, the achievement of pleasure depends on
the fulfilment of his social duty, but the fulfilment of this
duty is based on wealth. For this reason, virtue and pleasure depend on material goods.* (Artha Shastra, 1.2)

Success in life first requires the means of success, which include a minimum of acquaintances, material goods, and social
position. Only having these can a man dedicate himself to purely
spiritual values.

The pretense of despising material goods is a mere romantic
dream. None can truly disengage himself from the temporal aspects of life. The worker does not despise his tools, nor the scholar
his intelligence and memory. Rather, they regret not having better
instruments or keener intellectual faculties in order to improve
their work. In this world of action, all means for amplifying action
are important, and we must do our utmost to acquire and develop
them:

*This is a world of action in which work is glorified.
Agriculture, cattle-raising, and craftsmanship all con-
tribute to the creation of wealth. The sacred books tell
that without material goods, we may neither fulfil
our duties nor realize our desires. . . . A rich man is able
to perform his duty and obtain what he desires, which a
man without means cannot do. It is said that virtue and
pleasure are the by-products of riches. Without wealth,
nothing is possible.* (Mahabharata)

The acquisition of material goods rests on ten basic factors,
which are known as the ten mainstays of life.

*The ten mainstays of life are: knowledge, know-how, food,
manpower, cattle-raising, trade, agriculture, thrift, inheritance, and finance.* (Siddhanta, p. 185)

100

To acquire and conserve material goods, to increase and utilize them, to distribute and enjoy them, a man must work, be prudent, reflect, and make no mistakes.
(Bhagavata Purana, *11.23.17*)

A man must never be satisfied with what he possesses. Fortune abandons the man who is content with what he has. (Somadeva Suri, *quoted in* Siddhanta, *p. 191*)

To the extent to which a man who has acquired material goods declares that he is satisfied and gratified to the full, in like proportion is his luck stricken and his fortune ceases to grow. (Magha, *quoted in* Siddhanta, *p. 191*)

Neither intelligence nor human virtues attract wealth. It is money that attracts money, just as one elephant makes it possible to trap other elephants. (Niti Vakyamrita)

Material goods are clearly not an end in themselves. If they are that for the ambitious man, it is at the cost of limiting his personality, as with the puritan, the man who only sees duty, or the dissolute man, who only seeks pleasure. The mystic, who seeks liberation, can attain his goal only after adopting the conditions laid down by the other aims of life, which allow him to pursue his aim without ulterior worries. Wealth enables him to discharge his human debts, the essential prerequisite to spiritual liberation. Because material goods are the basis of all realization, "the rich man is honored by all, and all esteem him, even those that expect nothing from him" (*Artha Shastra*, 258).

Even a poor man may inebriate himself with mysticism, but generally he is too busy warding off cold, hunger, or vermin to be able to dedicate himself fully to contemplation.

The poor man becomes stupid, says Kautilya; *He is despised even by his own wife.* (Artha Shastra)

A man of duty needs considerable means to cope with his responsibilities.

It is not difficult for a rich man to do good, because its implementation depends on wealth.   (Artha Shastra)

Virtue is a bourgeois luxury, requiring at the very least shelter from privation. The so-called monastic poverty of the Christian world is false poverty founded on important capital, which is often considerably more per person than would be necessary for material tranquillity in secular life.

The vow of poverty of monks living in a community is merely the collectivization of wealth managed by the group, a little like a kibbutz. It is not, nor can it be, an absence or rejection of material goods. The resources of the monasteries give the monks the possibility of a life dedicated to the pursuit of spiritual experience.

The life of the sannyasi, the wandering monk of India, is possible only because the whole of society is organized to support him. No Hindu family will start its meal without ascertaining that there is no sannyasi at the door, since he must be fed before anyone else.

All pleasures are based on riches. Houses, cars, comfortable homes, servants, musicians, women, delicate food—none of these may be obtained without "means." Even the most fleeting and least onerous of pleasures or comforts—whether a hired car, a hotel room, or a prostitute—still requires a certain amount of money.

Property is the foundation of society, and the basis for all individual or collective realization, both human and transcendental.

Society exists for the purpose of creating favorable conditions for the acquisition of material goods, wealth, and power, in turn allowing science, culture, virtue, religion, pleasure, and spiritual pursuits to flourish. The basis of social organization is thus mainly economic. Caste divisions and the need for ethics, rites, and religion are all based on economics, or at least facilitate economic development under favorable conditions, which is in turn conducive to the realization of the four aims of life.

In India, the acquisition of material goods is the subject of a special science, *Artha Shastra,* the "science of means," which explores the means of assuring economic and political development, through which possible activities are increased and the stability of goods acquired is guaranteed. The "science of means" thus covers the whole field of management, economics, justice, and government, as well as the art of prosperity.

The first texts formulating the principles of Artha Shastra are found in the traditional codes of ethics and politics, known as *smritis,* and in particular the smritis of Manu and of Yajñavalkya, followed by important passages of the Puranas and finally by more specifically political and economic treatises, such as Shukra's *Niti* and Kautilya's *Artha Shastra.*

Each of the aims of life must develop in harmony with the others. Virtue must not make us forget pleasure, nor should a taste for money and political ambition lead us to neglect the rules of duty. Theoretically, a person should pursue a particular approach to its utmost limits, concentrating for example on political reality without any moral considerations, just as poisons might be studied without being used for any practical purpose. Similarly, in analyzing the acquisition of power and material goods, the *Artha Shastra* may leave ethics entirely aside. Each subject must be studied for itself, without prejudice, since only in its practical application can one decide how far to go without jeopardizing the other aims of life. From such a point of view, the *Artha Shastra* may appear as an example of the most utter political amorality. The error of most current political systems in the West is that they make insufficient distinction between theory and practice, which inevitably leads to some form of tyranny.

According to the smritis, material goods are of four kinds: those that may not be given away, those that may be given away, those that may be accepted, and those that may not be accepted.

The following kinds of goods may not be given away: goods that have been placed in one's custody, money that has been borrowed or that has been lent to one in case of need, goods whose lack would be harmful to one's pleasures or interests, property that has not been divided or that belongs to one's children or wife, one's total possessions, whatever has been received as a gift.

Goods that may be given away are those which, apart from the above, are not indispensable to the well-being of the family.

Goods that may be accepted include the price of a sold object; wages for work rendered; money offered to an artist, poet, or scholar as an expression of admiration; gifts from parents or friends as a sign of affection; fees for services rendered; a woman's dowry; and rewards for meritorious services.

Goods that may not be accepted are those obtained from a defeated opponent; from a man in anger or under the effect of alcohol, madness, despair, illness, or suffering; from a dependent; from a child; from someone who is not entitled to do so; or as a reward for a criminal act. Money may not be received if offered as a joke, for a dishonest transaction, by deceit, or from a desire to injure, or if it represents gains from gambling or speculation.

THE ACQUISITION AND USE OF WEALTH

The means of acquiring wealth may be honest or dishonest, but the use of dishonest means is prejudicial to the enjoyment of ill-gotten goods, since pleasure depends on virtue. Honesty is thus an important quality for the stability both of society and of the individual. (Siddhanta)

He whose wealth is pure is truly pure, not he who purifies himself ritually by washing with mud and water.
(Manu, 5.106)

This is why the king may not fill his treasury with wealth gained by illicit means. (Shukra niti)

A king may take part of his subjects' riches, but must do so with moderation so as not to dry up the source, just as the kid does not drink all his mother's milk, nor the bee suck all the nectar from the flower. (Manu Smriti)

Fifteen evils arise from ill-gotten gains: theft, cruelty, lies, deceit, shamelessness, anger, vanity, pride, setting-at-odds, enmity, lack of trust, envy, greed, gambling, and other kinds of bad conduct. For this reason, the man who seeks his own good does not desire ill-gotten riches.
(Bhagavata Purana, *11.23.17-19*)

Even honest wealth is not without pitfalls and may poison human relations.

Money divides friends, brothers, husbands and wives, and parents. All unifying bonds of affection are destroyed by it. (Bhagavata Purana, *11.23.20*)

Wealth is also a source of temptation.

Man will abandon all for riches: his affections, his duty, his country. He may even kill his parents or risk his own life. (*Quoted in* Siddhanta, *p. 187*)

Possessions may be ill-used in two ways: by benefiting the undeserving, and by not benefiting the deserving.
(Mahabharata)

In order to enjoy happiness in this world and the next, possessions should be divided into five portions: one part for good works; one for glory (yasha); one for advantageous investment; one for pleasures; and one for family and dependents (svajana). (Bhagavata Purana, *8.19.37*)

A budget that does not give sufficient space for good works and pleasure is bad, as are gains made without due consideration for ethics.

There are only three possible uses for wealth: to give it away; to enjoy it, or to lose it (dana, bhoga, nasha). What-

ever is not given away or enjoyed, ends in the third man-
ner.   (Bhartrihari, Niti shatakas)

The miser reaps no pleasure from his riches. He does not
enjoy them in life and, not having fulfilled his duty, nor
will he profit by them when he is dead.
                              (Bhagavata Purana, *11.23.15)*

Like a leprous spot that destroys all a man's beauty, greed
destroys his lustre.   (Bhagavata Purana, *11.23.16)*

Wealth truly shines when others benefit from it.
(Nitivakyamrita *from the* Soma-deva Suri). The commen-
tator adds that by "others" are meant gods, sages, ancestors, men, parents, friends, birds, and quadrupeds, as well
as himself.   *(Quoted in* Siddhanta, *p. 190)*

Of the eighteen passions that are prejudicial to wealth,
ten stem from pleasure and eight from anger. The ten
passions arising out of pleasure are women, hunting, gam-
bling, laziness, indolence, wickedness, drugs, dancing, sing-
ing, and the playing of musical instruments. Those born
of anger are slander, imprudence, cheating, impatience,
ill-will, disorder, insult, and cruelty.

                              (Quoted in Siddhanta, *p. 197)*

On the social and political level, "means" covers a great number of subjects, of which only the most important will be dealt
with here. The first are the various sciences and technologies for
the development of industry and crafts, followed by cattle-raising,
agricultural practices, and commercial methodologies, and ending
with politics and the art of governing, which include a considerable number of subjects listed in the *Artha Shastra.*

Among the basic problems regarding the government of the
state, the first dealt with is the choice of ministers and the tests to
which they must be subjected to assure their integrity. Next comes
the selection and use of spies and secret police, the setting up of an
independent juridical organ to settle disputes between private in-

dividuals and the authorities, alliances and intrigues in aid of favorable factions in neighboring states, the police, and the personal security of heads of state.

The administrative problems listed include the setting up of municipalities, division of land, collection of taxes, control of officials, mines and manufacturing establishments, money, the price of gold, precious stones and other valuables, reserves, trade, forests, weights and measures, the calendar (days of rest and feast days), customs, control of textiles, control of slaughterhouses, control of prostitutes, sea transport, and cattle.

Military administration includes the definition of the powers of officers; control over the administration of cavalry, elephants, war chariots, and infantry; supervision of the building of fortifications; and army recruitment and equipment.

The main problems encountered in the administering of justice are the control of tax collectors, the duties of municipal officers, contracts, legal forms, juridicial conflicts, marriage contracts (mutual obligations, wife's property, compensation in case of remarriage, wife's alimony and pension, cruelty, incompatibility of character, wife's misconduct, adultery, forbidden transactions), vagabondage, kidnappings, laws of inheritance and division of property, construction and sale of buildings, disputes over land boundaries, land survey register, the destruction of pasturage, fields, roads, breaking of contract, debts, warehouses, regulations concerning slaves and wage-workers, sales and purchases, property, theft, defamation, assault, gambling, betting, and other minor offenses.

In addition to the above, problems dealt with include the claims of the working classes, the prevention of excessive merchants' profits, protection against national calamities, the surveillance of young criminals, arrest for presumed guilt or *flagrante delicto,* inquests in the event of sudden death, trials and tortures employed to extract confessions, punishments by fine or mutilation, death penalty with or without torture, rape of underage girls, punishment for false witness, the rights of the defense, and convictions.

The general problems of government comprise the increasing of state revenues and finance problems, the salaries of civil servants, the conduct of courtiers, consolidation of power, absolute sovereignity, war and peace, alliances, protocol, precedence among rulers, neutrality, peace treaties, violation of treaties, evaluation of enemy strength, conquest, various strategies, intriques, destruction of enemy resources, policies of dissension, and restoring peace in conquered territories.

Although these are only the main subjects dealt with by the *Artha Shastra,* they suffice to show that the great problems of state administration and economy have changed very little over two thousand years. In studying the methods propounded by the *Artha Shastra,* it is even somewhat surprising to see how little man has progressed in the art of social and economic organization. Indeed, the Muslim and European conquerors of India were never able to change the basis of the administrative system except in minor matters and generally with unfortunate results. It can be said, rather, that it was England whose structures were influenced by contact with India.

7 THE THIRD AIM OF LIFE

KAMA: PLEASURE, SEXUALITY, ENJOYMENT

Self-realization on the Sensual Level

PLEASURE

The third aim of life, self-realization on the sensual plane, is one of the four aspects of the human being's harmonious development.

> *"Pleasures" include the enjoyment of whatever is desired. Whatever pleases the senses, whether word, touch, sight, taste, or smell, is comprised by this definition.*
>> (Prema Vallabha Shastri Tripathi, Tritiya purushartha ka Vihangamavalokana, *in* Siddhanta,[1] *p. 249)*

In order to reach the final aim of life, which is transcendental consciousness, life itself is necessary. The body is a set of faculties,

---

1. Many quotations in this chapter are borrowed from the volume on the four aims of life (*Purushartha visheshanka*) of the Hindi philosophical review *Siddhanta,* published at Benares in 1956.

constituting and depending on the "ego," the instrument that allows the temporal being to approach timeless consciousness. The body is thus the basis of all realization. All its vital activities are based on desire, on a need to be satisfied, whether the need arises from hunger, thirst, fatigue, or sexual desire. The satisfaction of the need is indissolubly linked with pleasure; it is in itself a form of pleasure. Pleasure is thus one of the conditions of life. A man must keep his body happy and strong if he is to achieve his ultimate goal, which is a state of joy and permanent happiness. He must not forget, however, that his body is not himself but is only a vehicle, which he must look after with the same care and affection as a fine horse. If he ignores the body's pleasures and neglects to satisfy them, his body will betray him somewhere along his path and he will not fulfil his destiny.

> *Without a taste for pleasure, even a rich Brahman will not eat fine food; without a taste for pleasure he will not be charitable. Without a taste for pleasure, he will ignore the joys of the body. This is why pleasure is the basis of all the other aims of life.* (Mahabharata)

> *He who does not desire pleasure will not seek to enrich himself. Without desires, neither does a man desire to fulfil his duty. He who is without desire is envious of nothing. This is why desire is the most important thing.*
>
> *There has never been, is not, and will never be anything that seems superior to what we desire. Desire is the essence of all action, on which all notions of duty and wealth are based. Just as cream is the essence of milk, so pleasure is the essence of duty, the source of wealth.*
> (Mahabharata)

> *The oil is better than the seed. Butter is the best of the milk. Flowers and fruit are the best things in the forest. Similarly, pleasure is more important than virtue or riches.*
> (Mahabharata)

The merchant, the laborer, the gods themselves act only if their actions are linked to some satisfaction. For pleasure, a courageous man will brave the ocean. Pleasure has multiple forms, which imbue every aspect of the world. (Mahabharata)

A man without desires never achieves anything. Everything that men have created has been done through the search for pleasure. (Manu, 2.4)

The Cosmic Being created the world because by himself he knew no joy. He wanted to be two.
(Bridadaranyaka Upanishad)

On the physical, as on the intellectual and spiritual plane, all creation, all invention, all imagination is the fruit of desire. People always recount events as they wish them to be, and it is thus that legend and history are created. Understanding this achieves what no rule can define. According to Kalidasa, it is necessary to understand the place, the means, and the situation, and then do whatever is most agreeable.
(Madhavacharya, Sakala Purusharton kasara,
in Siddhanta, *p. 266*).

Although sensual pleasure is experienced through the various sensual organs, the pleasure that really deserves its name is erotic.

The sexual organ is always the ultimate source of pleasure.
(One of the Upanishads, quoted in Siddhanta, p. 264)

The essence of a kingdom is its territory, of which the cities are the jewels. The best thing in the city is the palace, of which the best are its beds. The best thing in a bed is a woman, without whom the rest is worthless. (Rudrata)

111

PLEASURE AND THE OTHER AIMS OF LIFE

As has already been seen,

Pleasure is only easy where social and economic circumstances are favorable. In seeking to realize himself and in fulfilling his desires, each clashes with the desires of others. This is life's battle. Such a state of perpetual conflict can only be avoided by mutual agreement, by a set of conventions to which all subscribe for their own convenience. Respect for such conventions is known as ethics or duty. The pursuit of pleasure is made possible by self-imposed limits, which in turn make it possible to lead an agreeable and organized collective existence. As with forms of wealth, there are also forms of pleasure which run counter to duty, and upset the balance that makes the pursuit of pleasure possible, of which intrusions into others' pleasures are an example. This is why . . . it is wrong to entertain a desire for another man's wife.

(Shukra Niti)

When limited by duty, wealth and pleasure become sources of interior progress, whereas otherwise the quest for wealth leads to dishonesty and conflict, and the desire for pleasure to disorder and instability.

(Ramaprasada Premashankar Bakshi, Dharmaviruddha Kama, *in* Siddhanta, *p. 277*)

Where duty and money are not to be found, the word pleasure loses its meaning. (Shukra Niti)

Man must seek intensity in pleasure as he seeks abundance in wealth, and perfection in the exercise of duty. Ambition is the secret behind all progress.

One should always think, "Could I not do better in virtue, in riches, in love?" The success of life's journey rests on this attitude. (Shukra Niti)

112

Excess in pleasure, however, risks drying up the source and thus negating pleasure, so that moderation is recommended to maintain a balance in the aims of life.

> *The field forced to produce too much grows barren. Seed no longer germinates there and whatever is sown dies. Similarly, whoever gives himself over to excessive pleasure ends by losing it entirely. The fire flares up when oil is poured on it drop by drop, but is extinguished if the flow is too strong.* (Bhagavata Purana, 7.11.33–34)

In all the aims of life, there are imperfections, shortcomings, defects, mistakes, and weaknesses, which must be remedied. The main defect in love is the excessive importance attributed to it and its consequent illusions *(moha)*.

PLEASURE AND LIBERATION

The extreme sensation of pleasure is considered to be an image or reflection of the infinite ecstasy of the individual united with the universal or divine Being.

For many people, perhaps even for all, the discovery of divine reality is linked with physical love. All life's suffering seems to vanish in marvellous joy in the very first sexual act of adolescence, in which the first direct notion of the divine is often experienced. "God must exist, since so much joy is possible"—a notion that will remain fixed in the memory forever and is the source of all religion.

The thrill of intense happiness felt during the sexual act, making man unconscious of anything else for an instant and unmindful of all reasons, concerns, and prudence, totally abandoning himself to an inundating light of joy and an unparalleled bliss that fills his very being—this thrill resembles the state of ecstasy described by mystics of all religions when they attain contact with the divine lover.

Woman is the image of Nature (Prakriti), and man is the

113

*image of Being (Purusha). When they unite, they dissolve
into divine unity.   (Quoted in Siddanta, p. 275)*

For this reason, mystics always use a vocabulary of physical love, since there are no other words to describe this phenomenon. The uniting of two bodies and the resulting spark of joy is truly the reflection of the soul's union with God. How else, moreover, can the nature and effects of love be explained in a universe whose every aspect is coordinated and interdependent? Love is not only the reflection of divine union but also the path that leads to it. This transitory and free act, involving the total giving of self, and absolute oblivion with regard to human interests and worries, demonstrates their worthlessness and prepares man for renunciation and for indifference to the social values of daily life, without which he cannot detach himself from earthly ties. The wasteful agitations of the mind and reason preventing man from perceiving the inner light can then be effortlessly cast aside.

Mystics are erotic. They intuitively and profoundly understand the sensual pleasures of sexual love and prefer their experience of the divine merely because it is more delectable, more durable, more complete. It is the ambitious ones, not the mystics, who seek to place obstacles on the path of sexual love, since eroticism may become the means (perhaps the only one) of attaining liberation. There is a difference between the temporary and partial union of two living beings and the absolute and unconditional union of the human and the divine, but the sensual pleasure remains the same. Whether it is an instant in time or a timeless eternity, the desire and the form it takes are identical, marking the human being in the same fashion. It is impossible, however, to attain absolute pleasure, which like total liberation can be aimed for but never reached. For it to be reached, in fact, a state of unqualified nonduality must be attained, excluding the illusion of the world, an instant during which nothing but joy any longer exists. At such a point the self would cease to exist as an individual being. So long as the feeling of being distinct—of being two—remains, and the mind's agitation has not been stilled, the attraction and fusion will not be

114

complete. In pleasure, as in liberation, the illusion termed the real world must no longer exist.

If illusion does not vanish and the world cease to exist during contemplation, or spiritual or physical union, then the contemplation, or union of bodies or minds has failed.
(Quoted in Siddhanta, *p. 267)*

As the Hindi poet Sura Dasa says, "As long as your desire is not ardent enough, and the garden of the world still stretches before your eyes, veritable pleasure and the joys of divine union will remain beyond your grasp."

In fact, we seek pleasure because it reflects the happiness and joy that dwells deep within our nature.

Sensual pleasure is the image of the Being, the Atman.
(Quoted in Siddhanta, *p. 250)*

Because the barriers of the senses mask the true and absolute happiness of our divine nature, we are compelled to seek its image or reflection through our senses themselves. Pleasure exists for all beings, but only for man is it an aim of life, since for him it leads to further realization.

When limitless bliss (ananda) is attained, pleasure (kama) no longer has any meaning. Union (sangha) gives rise to pleasure, but its goal is joy. Eroticism is only a means.
(Patel Varigé, Siddhanta, *p. 275)*

This is why the *Kama Sutra* avers, "He who knows all the secrets of the erotic arts becomes chaste."

The difference between love and pleasure is that love is a static image of a state of eternal and unchanging happiness, whereas pleasure expresses the creative tension of the cosmos and is a participation in the work of Creation. Love makes two beings one and represents the fusion of opposites in the nonbeing and silence of the cosmic night. Pleasure separates two beings so that they can

115

try to identify with each other. It juxtaposes opposites, creating a magnetic current between them, which is the essential nature of all matter and all life. Furthermore, love is joy alone, while pleasure blends the joy of fulfilment with the suffering of desire. Love is the culmination, the annihilation of pleasure. Pleasure leads to love, which is the image of divine repose; whereas pleasure is the image of divine activity. Pleasure is thus simultaneously the path toward love and the obstacle to its realization. Love is a transcendent death, whereas pleasure is perpetual life.

All sensory organs are directed outward, which is why desire is directed to outward objects. Although pleasure is experienced as something inner and personal, it can be achieved only by union with an external object. Desire grows with the practice of pleasure, just as the desire for knowledge increases with study, and skill through exercise. We strive after total sensual pleasure, absolute knowledge, perfect skill but never grasp more than the outside. For this reason, progress in knowledge and pleasure must be organized like the higher realizations of man's estate, while still remaining at a human level. Such forms of progress approach man to the divine but very rarely to true identification with it. They are symbols or images, which gradually prepare man for transcendental realization, for a destiny beyond the human lot. This is why man's experience of pleasure and search for knowledge is limited and why physical pleasure and duty must stay in harmony, as long as we remain in a human state. We may thus attain the greatest happiness that either this world or the next can provide.

PLEASURE, THE INDIVIDUAL, AND SOCIETY

The perfection of human life consists in implementing to the full the four aims of life. Man must, however, realize himself not only as an individual but also as a member of a species or collectivity. The fate of the species as a whole is a part of the fate of each individual and cannot be separated from the realization of the latter. The individual's share in the realization of the collectivity is

116

called "participation in the sacrificial rite" (*yajña-bhavana*), by means of which mankind cooperates in the cosmic ritual of creation and realizes its function in relation to its creator—a function from which the individual may not and cannot dissociate himself, and which is expressed through religion, ethics, and rites. The individual seeking his own good cannot neglect the collective good of the group to which he belongs.

The quest for liberation and the performing of duty play a role that may appear obvious from the point of view of man's destiny in this world and the next. If life is viewed too narrowly, wealth and pleasure could be thought to concern the individual in his temporal life only. Such an attitude ignores the ritual value of all acts, which by their very nature have repercussions on the world outside, apart from any effect they may have on the development of the individual personality. The historical unfolding of mankind is the result of a multitude of positive acts that may appear unrelated but that have a collective value, like the bricks used to construct a building. For the artisan making the bricks, each appears stamped to a greater or lesser extent with his own personality, but in the construction of a great building, it is essential that each brick should be perfect. The artisan's personality is of marginal importance and appears as an entirely interchangeable element. Thus it is with all our acts. Every realization, each instrument of inner and outer perfection fashioned by the collectivity (although often unawares) constitutes the realization of mankind, from the babblings of infancy to the highest forms of knowledge. Even our most secret actions form part of this common work, playing a role in the building of the human edifice and of the work of creation in general, thus cooperating in the realization of the divine plan.

The quest for and realization of wealth and pleasure are not merely a search for personal happiness without concern for that of others. If we learn to consider all our actions, beyond all temporal and personal conditions, as a "participation in the sacrificial rite," a contribution of the human species to creation as a whole, we perceive that each of our acts has its own particular value, whether prayer, study, work, ambition, amusement, love, or pleasure. When action (karma) is seen to be a means of realization, it is conceived as a rite that bears no tangible results but contributes to the universal bank of actions (which on a more limited scale is what Christian philosophy terms the "communion of saints").

In the Hindu pantheon, the various aspects of the human being or god have existence, reality, and the power to manifest themselves only when united with their corresponding feminine counterpart, their Shakti, or power. The uniting of the phallus and female organ is the very symbol of the divine being's creative potential, as well as the cosmic and physical reality of creation. This union is the beginning and end of existence and the cause of its continuation. Because of its symbolic and creative value, the sexual act is the most important of rites and is performed as a rite. It is the most efficacious means of participating in the cosmic work. All other rites are but its image and symbolically reproduce the original union. Agni, the God of Fire and male principle, burns in the *kunda,* the altar hearth and image of the female principle. The Upanishads interpret all the aspects of sacrificial ritual as the various stages in the act of love.

> *Woman is the hearth, the male organ is the fire, the caresses are the smoke, the vulva the flame, penetration the ember, pleasure the spark. In this fire, the gods sacrifice semen and a child is born.*
> (Chhandogya Upanishad, 5.4–8)

> *The call is the invocation of the divinity. The request is the first hymn of praise. To lie down beside the woman is the hymn of glory. To lie face to face is the chorus. The climax is the consecration, separating the final hymn. . . . He who knows that this hymn of the left-handed god (Vamadeva) is woven around the act of love procreates himself anew at each union. He will live long, the whole length of his life. His offspring and cattle will be many. Great is his fame.* (Chhandogya Upanishad, 2.13.1)

THE FORMS OF EROTIC REALIZATION

Pleasure is one of the four aims of life and must thus be realized as fully as possible for the attainment of the highest summits of sensual experience. Contrary to the science of torture, which seeks to identify the points of the body that are most sensitive to pain, erotic science seeks the zones and techniques best suited for awakening intense sensual sensations. Erotic treatises first classify men and women into categories in order to pair the physical types best suited to each other, and then provide a systematic study of all the different kinds of sexual acts and their variations.

Erotic games may be extremely complex, with the participation of several persons. It is important for everyone to realize himself at this level, for so long as a man has not fully satisfied his secret desires and has not accepted the fact that such a satisfaction is one of the aims of life, involving participation in the natural order, he is incapable of accomplishing the other aims of life, in particular the final goal of liberation.

Pleasure (*kama*) and desire (*iccha*) are fundamentally of the same nature, the one being the fulfilment of the other. "I am the pleasure within all beings," says the god of the *Bhagavad Gita*.

Desire instigates pleasure. Desire is attraction, tension, the same that binds the stars and atoms. It thus expresses the very nature of all creation and is the sole permanent reality, whose temporary vehicles are the beings it possesses. Pleasure is the goal and fulfilment of desire.

Beauty and charm reflect universal harmony and are requisites for physical attraction. However, the harmony of living beings and their affinities are often hidden and mysterious. Erotic allure may be based on subtle inner qualities that are not revealed externally, which explains why love appears to invent and find qualities in a person who seems to be devoid of them: love perceives what an indifferent eye is incapable of. This is what the Vedantists term "creation of the eyes" (*drishtisrish-tivada*). The poet Majanun has written, "To see the beauty of Leila, the eyes of Majanun are needed," while the poet Bihari says, "Richness in beauty is measured by the desire of him that lusts after it."

Milk is unctuous, honey sweet, grapes are sugar, the rai-
sin sweeter still, but the sweetest thing of all is that for
which each man yearns.   (Quoted in Siddhanta, *p. 273)*

Eroticism is an essential aspect of self-realization. It belongs
to the transcendental, whereas the other aims—wealth and virtue—are classed as social and material values. Eroticism in itself,
however, is different from love and marriage, and these three distinct values should not be confused.

Marriage and the task of assuring a line of descent, although
constituting essential duties and a debt owed by each man to his
ancestors, do not necessarily or completely involve the experience
of love. Marriage is too tied to social and racial considerations to
include those aspects of selflessness and intoxication that are the
characteristics of pure love. A wife is the mother of one's sons,
which is what she is called. She is owed respect, affection, and
honor.

Marriage is a social institution, whose aim is the joint
fulfilment of the three temporal aims of life.
(Siddhanta, p. 276)

This does not necessarily imply total fulfilment. True love,
pure love can only be wayward and illicit. Love for what does
not belong to one (*parakiya*) is very different from love for what
belongs to one (*svakiya*). The first is true love and may become
the image of divine love itself. The mystics and epic poets idealize
illicit love as the only true one. Rukmini, the spouse of Krishna
and mother of his sons, is hardly spoken of, whereas his love
affairs with the milk-maids in the Forest of Herds (*vrindavana*),
and especially with his half-sister, Radha, are sung ceaselessly.

Love may assume four guises: it can be wonderful, ordinary,
degrading, or transient.

According to the *Sahitya Darpana,* using a classification in
vogue with most of the poets, there are three sorts of women:
one's own woman (*svakiya*), the woman of another (*parakiya*),
and the communal woman (*samanya*).

Modesty, virtue, and respect for her master are the adornments of one's own woman. Even if she is not his legitimate wife, she belongs to those worldly goods that bind man to this earth. More often than not, she represents comfort and agreeableness rather than passion.

The poets' ideal is the woman who belongs to another. She inspires total and unreasoning passion, which is difficult to bear and to fulfil. She is the image of mystic love: fugitive and difficult to hold, but knowing no limitations and without regrets. She inspires the giving of one's whole self.

The communal woman is encountered in gardens, public places, and temples, and her beauty seduces. Even if her lover idealizes her, it is but a fleeting love, since the communal woman is never either faithful or satiated and always seeks new adventures. She plays a very important role, though, since many men, even the least favored, can achieve through her one of the four aims of life, however temporarily and furtively.

For this reason, prostitution is sacred. It symbolizes the relationship between money and pleasure. The banning of prostitution is thus antimoral and antisocial, in the Hindu view. The prostitute's role is semi-sacerdotal, and if she performs the proper duties of her estate, she ranks high in the professional hierarchy. The Puranas mention several prostitutes who were celebrated for their intelligence, knowledge and virtues. The *Sankhya,* the great treatise on cosmology, refers to a certain Pingala, while in the *Bhakta-mala,* or lives of the saints, the prostitute Varamukhi is depicted as a model of absolute devotion.

This feature is not unique to India. In the history of every people and each civilization, "women of little virtue" can be found who have played an exceptional role, whether in the Bible or in Plato, as well as throughout the entire history of the Western world.

EROTIC ARTS AND TECHNIQUES

Erotic fulfilment exists apart from marriage and love. Marriage is a social function and love an exalted and even chaste friendship, whereas eroticism is a science and art related to yoga, and learned treatises explain its various forms and methods. These works form part of the education of every student in traditional schools. The best known is the *Kama Sutra,* but there are many others, and many chapters of the Puranas are also dedicated to the erotic sciences.

The texts on eroticism envisage seven kinds of attraction (*rata*): attraction arising from love, attraction arising from the performance, attraction arising from the occasion, indirect or imaginary attraction, self-seeking attraction, brute desire, and particular attractions.

According to Pandit Madhavacharya, when two lovers who are deeply in love have intercourse, their attraction is born of love (*ragavata*)—the attraction of true lovers that not everyone is given to know. This is the act of love with the most savor.

When a partial attraction is gradually built up during various attempts, it begins as a game, entwining and embracing and gaining an increasing intensity. This attraction arises from performance (*aharya*).

When two persons with different interests meet for some purpose, any intercourse they may have arises from the occasion (*kritrima*). Feelings on both sides may be pretended at first, but a certain attraction develops as particular qualities are discovered during the intercourse.

Each is enamored of another person, and only chance has made them meet. When they unite, each seeks in the other the image of the beloved, so that their attraction for each other is indirect (*vyavahita*), played as it were by proxy.

Water-carriers, servants, and women of low birth have a reputation for rapacity, desiring their wage immediately and never being satisfied. The tradeswoman seated in her shop is there for her merchandise and nothing else. These women have the same spirit as the whore, in that their desire, born of cupidity (*pota-rata*), leaves no place for genuine erotic feelings but is merely a question of work and pay. That is why this kind of pleasure is called "neuter" (*kliba*).

122

When a woman who is well versed in the arts of love gives herself to a peasant, such intercourse is termed rough (*khala*) or bestial pleasure, inasmuch as she cannot employ her arts, her partner being brutish. A man skilled in love who has intercourse with a shepherdess or an uncultivated woman finds himself in the same situation.

Particular attractions (*aniyantrita rata*) cover all other variations of love. In mystic love, every human being is androgynous and is both active and passive, lover and mistress at the same time, wholly penetrated by pure, immense, total sensuality. In his desire for limitless pleasure, the Creator formed women who love women and men who prefer men.

At the time of Akbar, the men who belonged to the sect of the *anubbashyas* were considered women and lived and spoke as women. Their master was Krishna, who was depicted as a virile man. Mystic cults devoted to Krishna have often encouraged states of sexual ambiguity in which all their adherents cultivate their feminine nature, in order to draw closer to the divine lover.

According to the *Rasa Panchadhyayi,* a man who at his death abandons his gross but completely feminized body, which has forced him to live separated from Krishna, because of his devotion acquires a body of pleasure (*ananda-maya deha*). By its means he will enjoy endless delight in the arms of Krishna, skilled in all the arts of love.

In ancient times, many men lived as women, dressed as women, and shared the life of the harem.

The mutual feelings of people who have known each other for a long time and trust one another entirely are influenced by each other. They form an indivisible unity in which contrasts no longer exist on the external level. It is at this point that friendship turns into love. Many homosexuals belong to this category, in which friendship, trust, and intimacy are also sources of love.

Complete trust in someone involves a simultaneous attraction or attachment, a relationship in which fear does not exist. The distrust and ignorance of mutual reactions that often separate the two sexes is absent, and pleasure becomes mutual and indivisible, like all life's other activities.

(Pandit Madhavacharya, Sakala Purusharthon ka sara-Kama, *in* Siddhanta, *pp. 267–268*)

According to architectural treatises, a love chamber (*rati mandala*) should be constructed at the top of the house, with a large bed and flowers and the walls decorated with erotic paintings, to which the master of the house will withdraw for amorous dalliance. All the old houses of Benares still have a room of this kind. The love chamber is sometimes a pavilion in a garden, which is better suited for passing adventures.

The Puranas and the *Kama Sutra* speak of eight forms of the erotic act: thinking of it, speaking of it, flirting (*keli*), looking at each other, speaking in secret, deciding to do it, the attempt, and consummation.

The contrary of these eight acts is called chastity.

(Agni Purana, *372*)

Erotic postures correspond to the related yoga positions, whose use is important for rich and poor alike. Only among adolescents can acts be easily improvised or technique be of little importance.[2]

According to the *Kama Sutra,* women of the doe, mare, and elephant types couple well with men of the rabbit, hare, and horse types respectively, due to the corresponding size of their organs.

Temperament may be of three sorts: lively, sweet, and average. Although badly matched temperaments can be adjusted to a certain extent, the same is not possible with physical types.

---

2. According to Indian doctors, female sexual inhibition is unknown in the case of child marriage. It is frequent, however, if the husband of the child-wife is considerably older.

*In love as in mystic union, unless orgasms are synchro-
nized, the feeling of identification which is the true consummation of physical love is not achieved.*

(Pandit Madhavacharya, *in* Siddhanta, *p. 273*)

*Bihari speaks of sixty-four elements constituting the erotic
act, which are hugging, kissing, scratching, biting, pen-
etrating, sighing, inversion (ranging from virility in women
to male homosexuality), oral coitus, making eight forms,
each with eight variations.*

*The eight types of hugging are divided into two groups,
according to whether they can be performed in public or
only in private.*

*The first serve to show affection, and are known as
touching, stroking, rubbing, and embracing, whereas those
which cannot be performed in public are the creeper, the
tree-climb, oil in the rice, and the churn.*

According to the Kama Sutra, *"the creeper" is based
on the Vedic text "Hug me as the creeper wraps itself
around the tree," the act comprising the man's pressing
against the woman and taking her lips with his.*

*In the "tree-climb," one of the woman's legs slides
along the man's, and the other encircles his waist, her
body pressed against his, lips against lips.*

*The last two forms of hug comprise the uniting of the
sexual organs, the latter being the symbol of infatuation
and passion.*

(Pandit Madhavacharya, *in* Siddhanta, *p. 273*)

Suvarnanabha adds to these last two the squeezing of the
thighs, the squeezing of the pubis, the squeezing of the forehead,
and labored hugging.

Of the kisses, the first three, according to Kalidasa, are "those
in which the lips are not parted" and are known as causal (*nimit-
taka*), blooming (*sphuritaka*), and widening (*ghattitaka*). The others are called equal (*sama*), inclined (*tiryaka*), illusory (*ud-bhranta*),

pressed (*avapidita*), and drawn in (*akrishta*). Games are sometimes played with kisses for stakes. Stealing a kiss by taking advantage of drunkenness or sleep is considered a punishable offense.

> *Sighs are part of sexual approach, and are also used in the extreme expression of pleasure, during penetration, and in hugging. Sighs are mingled with scratching and biting, taking in all sixteen variations.*
>
> (Pandit Madhavacharya, *in* Siddhanta, *p. 273*)

In a play by Subhasha Chandra Vasu, the heroine is made to say, "My father was of good family, but my mother was a woman of pleasure. When, as a little girl, I was taught all the paths of nonvirtue, I did not like it at all. I asked myself, 'How can I bring myself to do it?' But then, I got so used to putting up with these nuisances that I could no longer do without, and none of the ways of amusing men ever seemed difficult to me again."

> *Girls are led into pleasure by their girl-friends, their fos-ter-sisters who have already had some experience, their maids, women of ill repute, old servants, their elder sis-ters, and their confidantes.* (*Vatsyayana,* Kama Sutra*)*

> *To overcome modesty, drunkenness is useful, but is apt to be followed by remorse.* (Siddhanta, *p. 275*)

There used to be a great number of treatises devoted to erotic realization in India. Most have been lost, although many could probably still be found in scholars' libraries. The most ancient of these treatises are attributed to Dattaka, Nandikeshvara, Charayana, Suvarnalagha, Gothakamukha, Gonardiya, Gonimukha, Kuchamara, Virabhadra, Pururava, Bharata, Dandin, Jayadeva, Shamaraja, Shekharacarya, Minanatha, Damodara, Badarayana, Babhravya, Canikaputra, Shvetaketu, and Pancala.

Among published Sanskrit treatises, mention must be made of the *Kama Sutra* of Vatsyayana, the *Ananga Ranga,* the *Madana Mandira,* the *Rati Rahasya,* and the *Kama Kutuhala.* To these should be added the *Madana Tilaka* by Chandraraja, written in 1075.

8 THE FOURTH AIM OF LIFE

MOKSHA: LIBERATION

Self-realization on the Spiritual Plane

LIBERATION

To free ourselves from suffering and death and reach happiness is the conscious or unconscious aim of all our instincts and all our efforts. Our interest in anything is limited to the extent it can abolish sorrow and produce joy, pleasure, and happiness. For this reason, the supreme aim of life is inevitably conceived as an experience of absolute happiness and total joy, representing union with a transcendental being who can only be joy, beyond all suffering and death.

> Liberation means the abolition of all ties and all suffering. (Quoted in Siddhanta, p. 356)

Because we conceive of happiness in this life as total union with another human being, we also conceive of infinite happiness as union with a divine being. The notion of mystical union is based on the concept of physical pleasure.

Human beings feel incomplete, imperfect, and unfulfilled; they

127

are under the illusion that what they lack can be found in another human being and that the total union of two beings will form a perfect self-sufficient being. They forget that only the current of attraction uniting the two persons has permanent and eternal value; the two poles of the attraction are merely perishable objects of no importance.

Only the conviction and belief in a divine being whose nature is pure joy can justify the abandoning of all the transitory achievements of human life in order to seek a return to the causal state and freedom from the chains of creation, to the rediscovered equilibrium and unqualified happiness that is the very nature of the Creator himself.

The ultimate aim of transmigration and of life itself, for each living and transmigratory being, is thus the return to the causal substratum, the cessation of all individual existence, total dissolution in the absolute being.

Each human being lives enclosed in the cycle of his actions, and it is by means of these very limitations that the world exists. Trying to liberate oneself through purely personal efforts appears contrary to the natural order of creation. It is a partial foretaste of the end of the world and the cessation of the Cosmic Dream. Indeed, creation would effectively disappear if each individual cell managed to liberate itself and return to the causal substratum. Striving to attain liberation signifies, in reality, escaping from the divine play of creation and reintegrating with the divine person, thus becoming the enemy of the creative principle, nullifying its game and destroying its dream.

The whole organization of the natural world thus tends to prevent such a return and to keep within the play of forms these impermanent toys, reflections of the transcendental being, which are mankind. Liberation is the fruit of an incessant battle between Nature and everything in this world that seeks to last, perpetuate itself, and live. The gods do not like men to escape them and free themselves from the bonds of creation.

Living beings are useful to the gods, just as cattle are useful to men. It is unpleasant if even one animal is lifted.

128

So it is with the gods when men attain knowledge.
(Brihadaranyaka Upanishad, 1.4.10)

The created world must one day disappear and the manifested dream dissolve in the night of sleep. The worlds will vanish as they appeared, returning to the formless substratum. But the man who does not wish to await universal dissolution, enduring thousands of existences, sufferings, and deaths, may, through his own effort, put an end to the game, detach himself entirely from the world, and gain the impersonal beatitude of non-becoming.

Liberation is the essential meaning of life, because it alone leads beyond death. (Karapatri, *in* Siddhanta, *p. 36*)

To the very extent that they are divinely inspired, religions must make every effort to close the gate of liberation. Dogmatism is their main instrument, since only an unprejudiced spirit unfettered by belief can attain universal knowledge. Liberation is man's highest attainment, which he must accomplish alone, against the world and against the gods. Religions keep him in the chains of creation, replacing his search for freedom and transcendental intuition with the bonds of faith, which paralyze the flight of his thought and lead him to the half-truths of appearances and to the illusion of an eternity for his personal ego. By its very nature, faith is the contrary of knowledge. As soon as something is known, there is no longer any need to believe in it. This is why the abandoning of all religion, all ethics, and all the apparent values of the world is an essential condition of liberation to the Hindu.

"Renounce all religion and take refuge in me alone," says the god of the *Bhagavad Gita*.

DEGREES OF DIVINE UNION

Liberation has to be envisaged in two stages. Religions usually consider only the first and metaphysics only the second. It may be that both stages are realities and follow each other in succession, but the first may also be merely a decoy, a pious fiction created to

129

divert man from liberation and make him patient and less fearful of death. Religions postulate that the first stage never ends and that the soul remains individual even in its union with the divine, which for them is essential if their psychological, social, and moral action is to be effective.

The first stage assumes that the subtle being constituting the human individual can exist after death. This individuality, which survives physical death, is known as the transmigrant body and comprises the five principles of the senses; the five principles of vital rhythms; the mind, or thinking organ; the memory; consciousness; and the notion of self.

If these elements do not remain connected and cannot function on the subtle plane without the physical organs of the body that served them as a vehicle while alive, it is clearly absurd to talk of survival. A ghost or spirit that perceives nothing, thinks nothing, remembers nothing, and has no notion of its individuality cannot be considered a being. If it is a mass of some amorphous subtle substance, it is at the same level as the soul of a stone—or even less, since the stone's matter reacts to heat and cold and possesses the rudimentary reactions leading to sensation, consciousness, and life.

In the second stage of liberation, the individual entirely dissolves in the causal substratum. First his body returns to the matter that will serve to form other bodies. In the same way, his mind reunites with the cosmic mind and his consciousness with cosmic consciousness, to be used again in the formation of other beings until creation itself ceases and each of these aspects of the being dissolves in turn in the common substratum. The knot that binds and forms the notion of self is loosed and ceases to exist at the very moment of the death of the physical body, or of the subtle or transmigrant body. The second stage of liberation is thus a return to the causal substratum and the complete dissolution of the individual. The subtle being survives no longer than the body, except insofar as its mental or intellectual substance can be reemployed in other individuals, just like the mineral and even organic elements of the physical body.

According to mystics, there are four degrees in the union of the individual being with the universal being, which in the mystic's experience appears as a personal being and is called God.

The four degrees consist of being in the same place (*salokya*), the same world, the same heaven; of being close (*samipya*), contemplating the divine being, being in the presence of God; of having the same form (*sarupya*) as the divine being and of identifying oneself with him; of being united (*sayujya*) with the divine being, of no longer being separate from him.

The first three stages assume a survival of the individual, while only the last implies a complete return to the causal substratum and the dissolution of the independent entity of the created being.

The first three stages represent an inner experience for the human being and may give rise to the illusory hope of individual survival after death. To the Hindu philosopher, only the fourth stage appears as a certainty.

TRANSCENDENT REALITY

The Cosmic Being's power of illusion makes us see a mental vision as a concrete reality and leads us to conceive of a material, tangible world floating in the divine substratum. The nature of the world and of man are not, however, what they seem to be, since our notions of them are based on our limited and oriented perception. The basic reality about human beings is not limited by time and space, sorrow and pleasure, or birth and death.

> *The living being is a particle of God, and is therefore eternal. His consciousness, without blemish and without artifice, is a mass of joy.*
> (Tulsi Das, Rama carita manasa)

(But) *knowledge is enveloped by ignorance, which keeps man in the world of illusion.* (Bhagavad Gita)

Our limitations are merely apparent and lead us to an imaginary picture of the world. A man may dream of tragedy and weep, just as a man enveloped by ignorance, by the limitations of his senses and thought, believes himself to be material, mortal, and doomed to sorrow. Only the blindness born of his limited perceptions makes him believe he is only a puppet on life's stage. Man's only bond is that he believes himself to be bound.

It is as difficult to tell when the illusion known as life's reality began as it is to say when time and space began. Our perception of the world is like a building made of mirrors that reflect each other, creating an apparent infinity whose real dimensions can never be determined by our senses. One thing only can be said with any certainty: the bonds with which we are enchained—the limits of space, time, dimension, life, and consciousness—have existed only in relation to our perception. They are an appearance, the invention of what might be termed antiknowledge, or ignorance.

In transcendent reality, there is neither end, nor beginning, neither obstacle, nor effort, nor person seeking to liberate himself nor anyone who is liberated.
(Mandukya Karika)

The bonds that tie us to the world exist only so long as we believe they exist, as long as we believe we belong to the world. It suffices to lift ourselves above the world and leave it to see its falsehood, materialism, and suffering immediately disappear. (Siddhanta, p. 322)

Liberation is merely the renunciation of the false facts born of ignorance. It is the fruit of knowledge, an understanding that allows us to pass beyond the evidence of our illusory perceptions and see through the blindness of our senses. Wherever there is ignorance, liberation is impossible.

All man needs for self-liberation, therefore, is to realize his own basic nature, which can be termed his causal or spiritual nature: what he really is and not what he appears to be through the senses.

Knowledge leads us to recognize the illusory value of human

ties and the apparent realities of the world in general and to perceive the nonduality of the individual and the universal soul. The passage from individual to universal is not without problems, since identification with the causal principle is at the same time identification with everything that is created. The divine cannot be known without simultaneous knowledge of its works and manifestations, nor can we know God without at the same time knowing all God's creatures. Man must unite with the divine without at the same time melting into the whole of creation. Knowledge, which is the path to liberation, is also the most solid of the ties between man and the world, as well as between men themselves.

In approaching transcendental knowledge, man's individuality and human persona cease to exist. Knowledge of the universal soul and the obscurity of the individual power of realization of a particular human being are fundamentally contradictory notions. Wherever the universal principle is realized, the fundamental unity of creation and unity between all beings appears at the same time. No ambition for personal realization is thus possible. The integrated person identifies himself not only with the transcendent being but with all created forms and all living beings. He carries all humanity with him on his spiritual journey, and in this way he reintegrates with the divine.

Although liberation at an individual level apparently concerns only the person involved, it also profoundly concerns the whole species and the manifest world.

The living being plunges into the joy of the divine form which illuminates itself. Nothing else exists any longer. The person thus realized draws with him all those that approach him.　　　(Quoted in Siddhanta, p. 323)

From the world's point of view, the experience of happiness appears as a strictly personal realization. Even if they make use of external instruments, happiness and pleasure do not reside in these instruments but are an inner, personal, incommunicable experience. The self and enjoyment or happiness have to be defined in the same terms. They are not separate realities. The ego, joy, pleasure, and happiness are the indivisible object of our love, unconditionally and without limits. External objects, the instruments of our joy, the "you" can only be the objects of a qualified and limited love.

(Karapatri, Kama aur Moksha, *in* Siddhanta, *p. 324*)

QUALIFICATIONS

We must now see which human beings are capable of attaining liberation and of drawing others in their wake—those who are qualified to seek liberation, who are ripe enough to detach themselves from the tree of life. Apparently, the development of our own nature and the acquisition of knowledge allow us to detach ourselves from the interests and relative pleasures of the world and make the wise man ready to free himself from them. From the point of view of human thought and action, knowledge appears to be a strictly negative tendency.

The sage desires neither to live nor die, but bides his time as a servant awaits his wages. (Manu, 6.45)

He who is interested in neither vice nor virtue, nor wealth, duty, nor pleasure, who is free from the fear of sin, indifferent to both futile and important matters, as well as to pleasure and sorrow, has already realized himself.
(Mahabharata)

He who renounces duty, success, and pleasure and no longer desires anything, attains liberation.
(Mahabharata)

Having paid his three debts (to the gods, the sages, and to his ancestors), he must direct his spirit toward liberation. He who seeks liberation without paying his debts is certain to fail. . . . He who relies on your charity, whose actions have borne fruit, who pros-

134

trates himself before you in thought, word, and deed, he alone is ready to seek liberation.

(Bhagavata Purana)

Cosmology (Sankhya) considers liberation as the result of the direct and immediate perception of the very structure of the created world, namely the twenty-five "constituent principles" (tattvas) of the world, and thus closely bound up with knowledge. The constituent principles of the world are defined as the nonmanifested (avyakta), intellect (buddhi), the notion of self (ahamkara), the five principles of the elements (maha-bhutas), the five senses (tanmatras) (hearing, touch, etc.), the eleven sensory organs, which are the five organs of perception (ear, skin, eyes, tongue, and nose), and the five organs of action (mouth, hands, feet, sex, and anus), with the eleventh, which is the mental organ (manas), to which is added the twenty-fifth of the constituent principles, the person (purusha).

Others consider liberation as the vision of the universal soul obtained when man has pierced the five envelopes (maha koshas) containing the individual soul. The five envelopes are the physical body, made of nutrition (anna-maya kosha), the vital envelope (prana-maya kosha), including the five organs of perception and the mental organ, the intellectual envelope (jñāna-maya kosha), also involving the five senses of perception but associated with the intellect (buddhi) and last the spiritual envelope, or envelope of joy (ananda-maya kosha).

(Svami Svarupananda Sarasvati, Avasthatita chaitanya-tattva, in Siddhanta, p. 336)

THE PATHS OF LIBERATION

The attainment of liberation cannot be separated from knowledge, but in the first stages of his struggle to overcome the forces of the natural world and the magnetic power of creation that tends to imprison him within his cycle of existence, the adept finds several paths open before him: knowledge, action, and love. In a way, these three paths are related to the first three aims of life and express their essence. They are also connected with the three fundamental tendencies that form the substance of nature and the world.

Knowledge, like duty, has the same nature as *sattva* (the ascendent tendency).

Action, like wealth, has the same nature as *rajas* (the revolving tendency).

Love, like pleasure, has the same nature as *tamas* (the descending tendency).

Knowledge

The path of knowledge lies through the intellect. When we understand the nature of creation and of the divine, we can draw close to reality and dissolve ourselves in it. All forms of knowledge direct us toward their causal reality, and it is by the strength of our thought, by refining it, and by its growing sharpness that we can pierce the veils of ignorance and illusion that surround us and attain the light of the spirit.

Worldly goods, pleasures, and duties then appear in their true perspective and lose their flavor. At such a point, we are ready to discard them and to enter on the path of inner silence and total renunciation. Once he understands the vanity and instability of appearances, the wise man has no other aim but to regain that peace and silence through the detachment of nonaction and nonthinking.

> *Meditating on the atman, fixed on it and living by it, having shaken the dust of evil from their feet, they go whence none return.* (Bhagavad Gita)

Action

The second path of liberation is the path of action, meaning ritual action and the acceptance of the ritual value of all our vital acts but also comprising techniques such as yoga practices. Indeed, through yoga exercises, postures, and disciplines, we can disrupt the vital rhythms and movements of thought that trouble the calm waters of the lake deep within us, in which the divine being is reflected.

In our inner silence, we can contemplate the divine being face to face and identify ourselves in him.

> *One day, a sage seeking immortality looked within himself and contemplated the Self face to face.*
> (Katha Upanishad, *4.1)*

Love

The third path of liberation is the way of love. Through our attachment or passionate devotion to divine symbols and incarnations, or even to human beings who are their image, we can, by the complete gift of ourselves, cross all the barriers of ignorance and appearance. This is the path of *bakhti,* of devotion and love. In troubled times and in the most adverse circumstances, love can always triumph for the less gifted. For this reason the path of devotion is considered the easiest and thus the most to be recommended in the Age of Conflicts, the Kali Yuga in which we are living. Love knows no caste but requires only aptitude, intelligence, and rites. Without any stops, it can lead the most humble and the least gifted to total identification and liberation. On the mystic path of love, the lover perceives the divine being directly through the objective of his love. Human love and divine love are not consciously separate. Poetry and music are its precious adjuvants on the path of love.

> *When the transcendent being is perceived, the heart's knots are disentangled, doubts are erased, and the weight of our actions is lightened.* (Quoted in Siddhanta, *p. 323)*

SAMADHI

Samadhi (union) means a state of almost total but temporary identification between the human and the divine being. Such a state has every appearance of sleep and sometimes even of death. An expert in yoga exercises can stop his breathing, his heartbeats, and all the movements of his thought and, motionless, contemplate within the cavern of his heart the image of the divine being, which gradually grows until it fills his entire being.

There are two forms of samadhi. The first is a temporary vision or perception of the divine, after which the suspended body returns to life; the person, already freed within by his experience, resumes his human activities and can communicate something of his vision. Such a person is known as a "liberated living being" (*Jivana-Mukta*).

In the second form of samadhi, union with the divine becomes absolute. Consciousness does not return to the body, which is not organically dead but is deprived of its soul and principle of life. The body may survive for some time as an automaton until all semblance of life stops and its matter returns to the earth. At the same time, the transmigrant body dissolves and the chain of successive lives is broken. The living being has, by his own effort, attained his goal.

In such a way, all sages, yogis, saints, and—as a rule—all sannyasis are expected to die, as well as all men who have fully realized the four aims during the four stages of life. When he desires to quit the world, the sage chooses a propitious hour according to the stars. He bids his disciples farewell and then, seated in the posture of realization (*siddha-asana*), he stops breathing and stills his heartbeats, entering into samadhi forever. A stone tomb is usually built around his body without touching him, in which his body often remains for years without corruption or crumbling into dust.

Samadhi is so frequent that the disciples of false prophets who have had the ill-luck to die a natural death have been known to bind the body with cord into the posture of a yogi, in order to make the death seem voluntary. Several of the over-popular prophets of modern ashrams have ended recently in this fashion.

9 THE FOUR STAGES OF LIFE

All cycles in the world we perceive are characterized by the number four, which is the number of the Earth. Like all things terrestrial, man's life thus divides into four periods—the four stages of life. All life has a springtime, summer, autumn, and winter, as also its morning, noon, evening, and night. These four periods of life are called "the four stages of action": the four *ashramas*.

For each of these four stages of life, man's duties, rights, and pleasures are different, and it is dangerous to try to skip any of them. Even a man who since childhood has been drawn to the monastic life, to that renunciation that is a characteristic of the fourth stage, must force himself to run the course, however hastily, of the stages of worldly life.

In the adolescent, detachment is harmful to the fullness of his development, just as licentiousness is in an old man.

The four stages of life are the quest for knowledge and experimentation; family life and the acquisition of goods; retreat into the forest and reflection; and renunciation and total detachment from the world.

THE FIRST STAGE OF LIFE:
THE QUEST FOR KNOWLEDGE (*BRAHMACHARYA*)

The first stage of life begins when the child leaves the women's quarters and receives his first initiation.

Brahmacharya can be translated as "wandering in the Absolute," *Brahma* meaning "Immensity" and being also the name of the cosmic substratum. The word also serves for "understanding" and even "knowledge." *Charya* means "to wander" or "to move."

A recent puritanical interpretation of the word *brahmacharya* makes it synonymous with the "chaste life of the student," which from a traditional point of view is incorrect. A single ablution suffices to purify the adolescent from sexual contact or acts. Only the social aspect of marriage is incompatible with brahmacharya, and among the Hindus, marriage is always independent of erotic pleasure, whose theory is considered as one of the major sciences. The *Kamashastra,* or erotic science, is one of the obligatory subjects for all students and, like the other sciences, is taught starting before the age of twelve. There is no stricture on adolescent experimentation with erotic games.

An adolescent may not consummate his marriage before he has finished his studies. For Brahmans, the ceremony celebrating the end of student life usually precedes the marriage rites, even though a first ceremony may have taken place well before. The student's obligation to live frugally and serve his masters is incompatible with the social and economic requirements of the married man. In practice, the age for marriage varies according to caste.

Having passed infancy, during which his mother acts as his first master, the child leaves the women's quarters and enters the world of men, usually toward the age of twelve. Henceforth, he will be treated as an adult. If he is to study, he will leave his family

140

and go to live with a teacher, his *guru,* on whom he will depend totally until he has finished his studies. For the first two castes (priests and princes), the teacher is a scholar; for shudras, a master craftsman. For merchants and farmers (vaishya) there are no rules, and the child does not necessarily leave his family.

Even today, children of traditional Brahman families leave their parents between the ages of ten and twelve and make their way alone, carrying a light bundle, to one of the sacred cultural centers, such as Benares, where they will seek a scholar known to their family. If this master already has enough pupils the new arrivals make their way to others until they find one who will accept them. A scholar may have up to a dozen pupils, who live in his house, serve him, and may even go begging to assure the group's livelihood.

Just as a man digging with a spade finds water, he who serves his master acquires the learning that his master possesses. (Manu, 2.218)

Man owes all the elements of his inner and spiritual development to the experience of others who impart to him the language he uses to organize his thought, his rules of behavior, the ideals that guide his actions, his notion of destiny, and the means of implementing it.

Everything we know, whether or not the teaching was voluntary and conscious, has been learned from a master or elder. The person of the master or guru (a word meaning adult, elder) thus plays a vital role in the training of the individual. Civilization, culture, religion, and society all depend entirely on the values taught by the elders. The whole of life is spent in learning. This implies certain duties toward those from whom knowledge is received, as also toward that same transmitted knowledge. At each stage of his life, therefore, man must not only learn but also teach. A man who does not teach is a mean thief, burying a treasure that does not belong to him. Until a man relieves himself of the burden of knowledge received by transmitting it to another who is worthy, he cannot liberate himself.

141

One of the great problems in life for whoever has received knowledge is to find a "worthy disciple" (*patra*) who deserves to receive this heritage. Relations between master and pupil, elder and younger (mentally and not physically, of course, since the guru may be a particularly gifted child and the pupil an old man) thus form an essential aspect of all intellectual or spiritual development, assuring that the transmission of knowledge runs parallel with that of life. Such relations are therefore a sort of chain of intellectual and spiritual initiation.

A man's first master is always his mother, whence the crucial role she plays and the particular regard in which she is held by both child and man. It is not merely that she has given him life, which is often a fortuitous accident, nor because she has nourished him with her milk, but because she is the one who initiates him into the society of man and who teaches him the first rudiments of language and behavior on which his whole future development depends.

A foster mother can often play the same educational role as a natural mother, and in polygamous Hindu society a father's several wives may share this function. According to Hindu ethics, a child owes equal respect and affection to all his mothers—that is, to all his father's wives—while the women themselves owe the same care and affection to all the children. This can sometimes raise serious ethical problems, such as the one that led to Rama's exile in the *Ramayana*. The story shows, however, that the greatness of the maternal role lies not in gestation but in the child's first training. A young wife of the old king, Rama's father, obtains Rama's banishment in order to make her son, Bharata, heir to the throne. Rama accepts his banishment because his duty demands that he show the same respect, affection, and obedience to this woman as toward his own mother. Bharata, however, will reign only in the name of Rama, his elder and the son of another mother. He recalls him from exile and restores him to the throne.

In all life's circumstances, man must obey and respect his mother. He may not, for example, become a monk without her express permission. She will always be his first guru, the first of masters.

142

During the first years of childhood, the father may play the role of advisor but never of master. He is the head of the family, and his preoccupations and duties are material and social. Family interest is more important than personal concerns, and a father is therefore never a sure guide for the individual's development.

For this reason, as soon as the child leaves infancy and the women's quarters toward his tenth year, he is placed in the hands of a master, or guru, whose life he shares and who fosters his intellectual development, his studies, and his professional apprenticeship.

Formerly, the most famous scholars often retired to the forest, where they continued their teaching. They set up a kind of farm, known as *ashrama,* where they practiced a little agriculture and cattle-raising to support master and pupils. As used here, the word *ashrama* denotes the third age, the "retreat into the forest," since this is the stage of life that applies most specifically to the meaning of "leaving off work" (*shrama*). One of the duties of men as householders during the second stage of life is, if they are wealthy, to make generous gifts to scholars. Thus there is always a source of income to support master and pupils without great financial hardships, somewhat like the great foundations set up by major industries today.

Knowledge may not be sold. As a result, teaching has to be free. Even a pupil from a rich family comes to his master with empty hands and never pays him. At the end of his studies he must make him a gift according to his means, which must comprise fruit, gold, and clothes. The gift can also be merely a symbolic offering. Other gifts such as cattle, land, or considerable sums of money may be added as well. However, it is always a freely given gift, which the master may not demand and for which he gives no thanks. He shows goodwill to his pupil simply by accepting his present, regardless of its value. Scholarly families sometimes acquire considerable fortunes and land in this manner. From the Hindu point of view it is not the giver who has to be thanked but the recipient who is willing to accept the gift, thus taking upon himself a part of the giver's debt—the debt owed by every man to his fellows and to the gods for all the good he has received or acquired.

143

For Brahmans, a student's life is severe, and the student living in his master's home has to observe the following rules:

He must master himself and develop endurance. He must bathe each day, be clean, make offerings of water to the gods, sages, and his ancestors. He must worship the gods and put fuel on the sacred fire. He must abstain from honey (liquor), meat, scent, garlands of flowers, spicy or sour food, and must eschew cruelty to any living creature. He must not use ointments on his body, or eye-drops for his eyes, nor may he wear shoes or carry an umbrella. He must avoid sensual pleasure, anger and covetousness, and may neither dance, sing, or play musical instruments. He must also refrain from arguments, gossip, lies, nor look at or approach a woman, or strike anyone. He must sleep alone and not waste his semen. He who discharges his semen too frequently breaks his student's vows.

(Manu, 2.175–180)

The rules are less strict for the other castes.

When an adolescent finishes his studies, he ceremonially puts on a pilgrim's garb and departs to visit the holy places before returning to his family and setting himself up in life. This ceremonial pilgrimage is today often a mere formality, but it is never omitted. Just before the marriage ceremony, the young man puts the garment on and takes up the pilgrim's staff. He then leaves through one door of the house and returns immediately by another.

Although his life as a student has now ended, the young man must again choose a guru, whose teachings he will follow, whose advice he will seek, and who will serve him as a spiritual guide throughout his life.

A man's last guru is always himself. There comes a moment when a man no longer has to listen to an external voice but to an inner voice, which alone can lead him to the highest reaches of spiritual life and beyond the gates of death itself.

144

THE SECOND STAGE OF LIFE:
FAMILY LIFE (*GRIHASTHA*)

Having lived with his master for the first quarter of his life, the "twice-born"[1] must live in his own house during the second quarter of his life, after marrying.

(Manu, 4.1)

The second stage of life is dedicated to domestic affairs. The word "domestic," from *domus,* house, corresponds precisely to the Hindu concept of the "Master of the house" (*grihasta,* from *griha,* "house"). The young man marries, meaning that the marriage is arranged by the two families, taking into due account caste, heredity, degree of relationship, physical type within the caste, and the matching of horoscopes, which is essential for a harmonious union.

Marriage is a social organization, whose purpose is the continuation of the race, the caste, and the family tradition. There is therefore no question of leaving it to the hazards of adolescent infatuation.

The Hindu couple rarely see each other before their marriage. Children are usually married before having had any sexual experience and, when they are old enough, find no difficulty in uniting. A first ceremony, which could be termed a betrothal, takes place between the children, the marriage being consummated as soon as the girl reaches puberty, at about twelve years of age. Brahman boys, however, may not consummate their marriage before finishing their studies.

The idea of seduction has no part in the psychology of the young Indian. He knows that a certain girl will be his wife and with curiosity and interest awaits the day when he will get to know her. For girls in particular, the whole risky game of hunting for a husband, needing to be seductive, and catching a desirable mate

---

1. As stated above, the phrase "twice-born" refers to members of the first three castes, whose initiation is considered a second birth according to a special rite.

by any means is nonexistent, making the Hindu woman very different from her Western counterpart.

The contrast in behavior between young girls and married women, so striking in the West, is absent in India. A Western-type courtship scenario is unknown. After a few years, while they are still adolescents, Hindu couples already have two or three children, fulfilling their social duty by assuring the continuation of the race, and paying their debt to the nation. They still have all their lives before them in which to meet adventure and know love in all its forms, without affecting the continuity of the family line in any way.

Marriage is arranged by families according to the rules of consanguinity, which vary according to caste and to the type to be emphasized. Blood ties on the mother's side and on the father's side are thought to differ greatly, and color is also considered of great importance.

> For the "twice-born," a girl who does not have a degree of relationship allowing her to attend funeral rites [i.e., a cousin not less than six times removed] and who does not bear the same family name as her fiancé's father should preferably be chosen for marriage and sexual relations.
> (Manu, 3.5)

This ancient rule is not always followed by many castes, however, and in some regions of India a young man must marry his father's sister if she is not already married.

> Matrimonial relations should be avoided with ten kinds of families, even if they are rich in cows, goats, sheep, money, and grain. Such families are those that do not observe the rites, who have no male children, who have no education, or else have hairy chests, or suffer from piles, consumption, dyspepsia, epilepsy, white or black leprosy. (Manu, 3.21)

However, the highly structured conventions of marriage in Hindu society do not disallow options for variations, eccentricities, and exceptions.

146

There are eight kinds of marriage. Priestly marriage (Brahma); the marriage of Gods (Daiva); the marriage of Sages (Arsha); of the Rulers of the World (Prajapatya) and Genies (Asura); of the Celestial Bards (Gandharva); of the Demons (Rakshasa); and of Evil Spirits (Paishacha).

(Manu, 3.21)

Priestly marriage is to honor an upright man, well-versed in the holy books, offer him clothing, and ask for his daughter's hand.

The gift of a girl covered with jewels to a priest who daily accomplishes his sacerdotal duties is the form of marriage called the marriage of Gods.

The gift of a girl according to custom, after having accepted from the suitor one or two yoke of oxen for sacrifice is called the marriage of Sages.

The gift of a girl after venerating her together with her fiancé and saying to them, "May you both fulfil your duty!" is the form of marriage of the Rulers of the World.

Receiving a wife after voluntarily paying her or her family a sum according to one's means is the marriage of Genies.

When girl and boy cohabit by mutual consent, it is called the marriage of the Celestial Bards. Its origin is desire, and its goal physical pleasure.

The form known as marriage of Demons consists of abducting a young girl, who protests and weeps, after having forced open her door and killed or manhandled her brothers and parents.

When a man couples in secret with a girl who is sleeping, drunk, or insane, it is known as the union of Evil Spirits. It is the eighth and vilest form of all unions.

(Manu, 3.27–34)

The first four forms of marriage are acceptable for Brahmans, while the demoniac form is acceptable for princes or warriors, and the form of marriage for Genies is tolerable for merchants and artisans.

Of the last five forms, three are valid, those of the Rulers of the World, of the Genies, and of the Celestial Bards, whereas two, those of the Demons and of the Evil Spirits, are invalid under our law. The forms of the Evil Spirits and of the Genies must never be practised. (Manu, 3.24–25)

The forms of marriage of the Celestial Bards and of the Demons, whether separately or mixed, are traditionally tolerated for warriors. (Manu, 3.26)

After marrying, the young couple must set up house. Starting from the marriage rite, they must keep a fire going in the hearth, which in the whole Indo-European world is the symbol and protector of the family group. This custom dates from the earliest period of the Aryan civilization, which still remembers the name of the men (*Ribhus*) who first procured and domesticated fire and made it the center of the home. During the remote ages of Vedic civilization, among the scattered populations of the north, fire was difficult to produce and caused serious problems when it went out, hence the magical importance attributed to tending the fire as a symbol of family unity. In certain very orthodox Brahman families, the fire used to cook food is the same one that was lit at marriage and has never been allowed to go out. It is considered bad luck for a fire to die: Agni, the god of Fire, has left the house. Many hymns in the *Rig Veda* are addressed to Agni, imploring him not to abandon the family that faithfully feeds and worships him.

A magical value is always attributed to the undying flame. Even today, there are still temples that have kept their lamps burning without interruption since their construction in the ninth and tenth centuries, greatly adding to their importance as sacred places.

In the Hindu family, relations between husband and wife are very formal and without intimacy. Families are patriarchal units, forming a numerous community, in which the women live in one part and the men in another. Intimacy between the couple is not possible during day-to-day life. They meet for a few minutes when, during the second half of the night, the husband enters his wife's room, or they find themselves together in the corner of a terrace.

148

Once the first half of the night has passed, one may go to the chamber of pleasure, washing one's feet before returning to bed. (Dharma Dipika, 43)

Only much later in life, when the master of the house retires from active life in order to retreat into the forest, does he really live alone in intimacy with his wife.

In castes belonging to the matriarchal system, the wife owns the house and land. Her husband has no rights and may well live outside the house.

Once married, the young man must set about acquiring material goods or increasing those he already possesses. The acquisition of wealth (*artha*) is a duty, because it is the source of pleasures as well as the mainstay of society and religion. Man must not neglect his well-being. Detachment and scorn for material possessions are not virtues but defects during this second stage of life. However short this stage may be, as for those destined for the monastic life, it must be gone through and the obligations it imposes honorably fulfilled.

The whole of society is based on the couple, the family, and property. The fullness of human life and the enjoyment of all its advantages form part of the privileges of the second ashrama. Jewels, comfortable apartments, gardens, music, amusements, dancers, mistresses—all these are the lot of this second stage of life. Each caste, however, has restrictions that limit these pleasures. Brahmans, as already discussed, have many more restrictions than other castes.

Just as great and small rivers wend their way to the sea, so do all the stages of life depend on the householder. (Manu, 6.90)

The student's life, family life, the life of the hermit, and the life of the wandering ascetic are the four stages of life, and for their livelihood, all depend on the married man. (Manu, 6.87)

149

THE THIRD STAGE OF LIFE:
RETREAT INTO THE FOREST (VANA-PRASTHA)

Having founded a family and prepared an inheritance for his children, the man who begins to feel old must devote himself to study and reflection.

When the master of the house notices the wrinkles on his forehead and sees his hair turning gray, when his son has a son, he must withdraw into the forest.

He renounces all he possesses and all nourishment coming from the products of labor in the fields. He leaves his wife under his son's protection, or else takes her with him, and departs for the forest. (Manu, 6.2–3)

There he must devote himself to study, to mastering himself and being kind to all creatures; he must meditate, be charitable, accept no gifts, be good to all. (Manu, 6.8)

He must not seek comfort. He must be continent, sleep on the bare earth and live under a tree, without considering that the place belongs to him. (Manu, 6.26)

Today, when forests are less accessible and more remote, many Hindus retire outside the town to a small house surrounded by a garden, living a life of retreat, visited by their children and friends, and spending their time in reading and philosophical discussion.

THE FOURTH STAGE OF LIFE:
RENUNCIATION (SANNYASA)

Having spent the third part of his life in the forest, he must become an ascetic during the fourth part, renouncing all attachments. (Manu, 6.33)

After several years spent in retreat and reflection, in the peace of natural surroundings, the aging man must then practise absolute renunciation. He leaves his aged wife, who returns to live with her sons, and dons the garment of a wandering monk. He departs alone, begging his food, journeying on foot from one holy place to another, spending the night in temples, or resting in the half-ruined houses surrounded by rank gardens, which pious people give over to these monks. In such a place the old man usually finishes his days. This period of life is called renunciation (*sannyasa*). The old monks spend their time in religious discussion, beg their food, cook a little, and assist the most aged among them. Young people often come to listen to their discourses and render them small services.

The duration of each stage of life varies considerably from one individual to another. Not all reach the fourth or even the third. Some go through the first stages very quickly. A young man drawn to the monastic life will marry very young and leave his wife almost at once. He may not, however, leave the world without first coming to know it, since no one can renounce what he does not have. One cannot take a vow of abstinence or poverty without knowing love and wealth. So much the worse for the girl whose stars and destiny have given her a future saint for a husband: she will spend her whole loveless life in the family of the husband who has abandoned her, and whom she will never see again. She will, however, be honored and respected as the fortunate wife of a great man. In contrast to the young sannyasi, many people relinquish life's pleasures only when they feel the approach of death.

The succession of the four stages of life is considered the normal cycle of human existence, but no Hindu will ever guess their duration. No social pressure forces a man into renunciation. On the contrary, the family group tries to hold back whoever is drawn to renunciation. Women in particular, who have only the secluded life of an abandoned wife to look forward to, do their very best to keep their husbands from renouncing the world. At the same time, quite a number of women take the orange robe and staff of the wandering monk and abandon husband and children. Such a woman was the famous Ananda Mayi of our own times, who in her ashram in Benares, merely by her presence, since she rarely spoke, brought calm, sweetness, and peace to those who were worried or in pain.

The fourth stage is not at all necessary for the attainment of sainthood, inner perfection, and liberation. All these stages are but the natural climate for the various ages of man, and no merit is obtained merely by conforming to them. Each person must first strive to to know his own nature and then pause at the physical, intellectual, and emotional form of life that best suits his equilibrium and allows him to realize himself to the full. This is the only true virtue.

There are countless sects of monks to suit all natures. They may be puritanical or licentious, practicing magic and erotic rites or the most austere virtues. The sannyasis, or monks, form a society outside regular society and fulfil a particular function. They are not in conflict with society, except perhaps in the rare cases of Tantric sects that practice ritual murder. Through the sannyasis the esoteric teachings of Hinduism are transmitted. Thanks to them, the secret meanings of texts and rites can survive all disasters and allow tradition to reappear when the right moment comes.

10 CONCLUSIONS

HINDU SOCIETY IN THE MODERN WORLD

Two main facts appear from the very beginning of any study on traditional Indian society. One is the very particular organization of society, which has been responsible for the balance that has enabled Hindu civilization to survive all invasions and to develop without revolutions or important changes, throughout more than four millennia, with a continuity that is unique in history. The other is the aptitude of this society to assimilate new elements, whether whole populations of conquerors or conquered, or technical, philosophical, religious, and scientific developments, corresponding to the successive contributions of the various ages of mankind. In our own time, this power of integration has been at work in the apparently rigid society of the princely states of India, which, while respecting the norms and principles of the Hindu hierarchy, adapted themselves more efficiently to modern technology than did the provinces of British—and subsequently Republican—India, where the attempts to destroy the Hindu social order have made modernization inefficient and aberrant.

Wherever modernization has taken place in the framework of India's traditional society, it has been easier, more effective, more complete, and more durable than when it has been tied to Islamic or Western-type social transformation.

A serious and impartial study of Hindu society shows that its principles are among the most modern and most adaptable in the world, enabling it to offer solutions to problems that plague other civilizations. Some aspects of Hindu society appear rigid to our eyes because for more than a thousand years it has withdrawn into itself as a result of successive domination by Muslims and Europeans, whose influences are still felt, the present governing class being entirely trained by Western standards. Until independence, only the princely states were in a position to maintain the essential bases of social order. This is no longer so.

Hinduism is a religion without dogmas. Since its origin, Hindu society has been built on rational bases by sages who sought to comprehend man's nature and role in creation as a whole. They organized society in such a way as to facilitate the development of each human being, taking into account his inner nature and the reasons for his existence, since for the Hindus the world is not merely the result of a series of chances but the realization of a divine plan in which all aspects are interconnected. An examination of the principles that have guided the organization of Hindu society may therefore be of interest. Instead of the slogans on which modern society seeks to build itself, we find an effort to try to understand social realities and the roles of the various races, as well as of the various kinds of human beings, in creation as a whole—an effort that alone can enable us to adjust to problems that would otherwise be insoluble.

In the Hindu view, the West has disseminated disorder and confusion everywhere by refusing to recognize the Creator's will in giving men different aptitudes, even going so far as to refuse to admit any difference in the duties, aptitudes, functions, and ethics of males and females, who are the very manifestation of cosmic opposites. For the Hindu, such leveling is indicative of the suicidal tendency of a species, inasmuch as the intensity of life is based on its wide range of differences, while leveling in any order of things is always the symbol of death itself.

It is not easy to explain the structure of one civilization in terms of another. Every social organization presents seeming injustices, unsolved human problems, and dissimulated or accepted forms of cruelty. We are easily shocked when the habits of other peoples differ from our own but remain unconscious of the defects of our own social structures, which are accepted as inevitable, in the pious hope that the future may find some solution for them. We usually seek to reform our institutions on the basis of political ambitions, which tend to replace one injustice with another, merely changing the status of the victims. The recent history of the West is most eloquent on this point.

If we do not know ourselves, we cannot understand the outside world. The key to the macrocosm lies in the microcosm, since it is only in our own being, by introspection, that we can finally attain access to the Cosmos, without being limited by the barrier of our senses. This is true not only for the individual but also for mankind collectively. Nothing can be understood about social man and his nature, behavior, real needs, and destiny without placing him accurately in the context of universal phenomena, without understanding the role and function of man in the world.

Hindu society is the result of an attempt to situate man in the plan of creation and to understand the nature and utility of his various aspects, including race, degree of development and mental possibilities, the diversity of individuals and their tendencies, and the implications of this diversity in intergroup relations. The society set up by the Hindus seeks to conform to a general order—a universal plan that governs the birth of worlds, the birth of life itself, the movements of the stars, and the currents of thought—that gives mankind a reason for being other than mere material progress from which only a few can benefit.

In the application of such a plan, if not in its very gestation, some errors of postulation may inevitably be made. Society realizes that these errors do not fully represent the real order of things or reflect the nature of the world exactly as it appeared in the mind of the Cosmic Being. It is probable that, more than any other, the Hindus' concept of society has taken into account the reality of the various human, material, mental, spiritual, individual, and social levels, while prudently avoiding the theoretical and imprecise speculations that have caused the decline and fall of other civilizations. The absence of dogmatism inherent in Hindu thought always leaves the door open to technical improvements corresponding to progress in discovering the subtle nature of the world and things.

In any society, rigid systems lead to abuse and injustice, but prudence is necessary to avoid rapid judgements. The same cruelties and inequalities are found in all social systems, because they reflect a particular aspect of the nature of creation and themselves belong to the nature of things. Such injustices are, moreover, more dangerous when they are wilfully ignored and considered accidental or inevitable. The only differences in the hierarchy of injustice, in the degradation of the human being, are usually merely of moment and procedure but are sufficient to make us all blind to the defects of our own social order and alive to those of others. For example, no society, even those practicing slavery, treats human beings with greater harshness and contempt for their inner dignity or with more vulgar tyranny than conscripts are treated in most European armies. Yet most citizens appear to find it natural to subject their sons—and curiously not their daughters—to this treatment against their own will. Should one of these military slaves revolt, should he have the dignity to strike a superior who insults him and forces him to perform useless and degrading work, he will in all probability pass the rest of his days in one of those charming rest homes known as convict prisons, unless he is shot, the war season permitting. The so-called pariahs of India have never been subjected to such outrage and have never been required, even temporarily, to strip themselves of their dignity and personality in such a way. In India, the military career is strictly reserved to the warrior caste, to which kings belong. This caste is the highest after the priestly caste, and its social privileges are a compensation for the risks run in defending the other castes.

Every civilization has professions that are more or less noble, or more or less disparaged. Only the method of selecting individuals for them varies, and it is not always easy to discern which is best. Street-sweepers are rarely invited to lunch with middle-class families, yet virtuous Europeans are often heard decrying caste injustice and the odious Brahman who will not share his meal with the butcher or allow the sweeper or the tanner to draw water from his well.

Contrary to what is taught on human equality, the Brahman believes that all men are equal in their possibilities and rights on the level of spiritual realization, but that on the human level each has a function, that they are born with different duties to fulfil and aptitudes that differ, and that such differences are not aberrations due to an irresponsible creator but correspond to the fundamental necessities of the species. It is necessary to understand these differences in all individuals if their earthly life is to bear fruit. By creating strict limits that take into account the various aptitudes of different men, Hindu society has eliminated an unequal free-for-all competition in which the weakest is always the victim. Caste society gives each man a place among his equals, after which the caste takes its place in society. Even if such a place is not much, it is impregnable and certain. In all cases it is much more comfortable and enriching than whatever the isolated caste could have created for itself in its environment and original conditions of life. The individual leaves his group only if he has sufficient merit to make himself a place above and outside the castes.

It should not be forgotten that the greatest poets, such as Sura Dasa, Kabir, and Rama Dasa; the most venerated saints; and the famous artists who sculpted the images in the great temples of India often came from the humblest classes of society.

The West can boast no advantage here, no effectual superiority. Wherever they survive in theoretically egalitarian societies, institutions like the castes always give such isolated groups, even when they are ill-treated and unjustly persecuted, the possibility of working usefully for the very society that isolates them. In this connection, one of the most important contributions by the ex-slaves of the New World to modern civilization—jazz—would probably never have developed if the blacks had not at the same time formed a separate caste by their work, playing a functional role in the development of American society. If they had been directly assimilated by white society, they might well not have contributed anything of importance to the culture of the United States or to the world in general. On the other hand, if racial groups are isolated, crowded into reserves like the American Indians or Australian aborigines, they can only atrophy and disappear.

Historically, all attempts to establish the equality of men without taking castes into account have led to the destruction of the weak by the strong—if not always physically, at least culturally, socially, and religiously. This is inevitable, since each group cherishes its institutions, customs, social laws, religion, culture, and language—and in fact thinks and acts like a caste. If one group is unable to impose its way of life and thinking on the rest, it can be sure that in a casteless society, sooner or later, it will see the triumph of the culture, religion, and customs of one of its adversaries, or at the very least a mixture will be produced and a compromise imposed. Islam, which in theory and doctrine recognizes no social or racial distinction in religion or state should, by definition, be the most democratic. In reality it has been the most intolerant and destructive. Wherever Islam has passed, only ruins and deserts can be seen and whole peoples annihilated. Presiding over the disaster is democratic Islam, which treats the few survivors of the civilizations destroyed, who have submitted body and soul to its physical and spiritual conquest, with a considerable sense of equality and justice. Of them it may be said what Tacitus said of the Romans: "They create a desert and say they have established peace." It was also to impose their ideal of equality, so profoundly contrary to that of liberty, that the Western peoples sought to impose their ideas, culture, religion, language, and ways of living and thinking on the peoples of their empires who preferred to live and think differently.

Whole races and civilizations have been destroyed by the European conqueror so that he can preserve the illusion of living in a world of justice, equality, and democracy. In reality, so long as the Western world does not take into account a system of mutual guarantees allowing different races, cultures, and religious forms to coexist, and prohibiting proselytism and mixtures, it will never be able to form nations or empires in which the various racial elements can collaborate without any of them feeling the need to destroy another or reduce it to impotence.

The apparent decadence of contemporary India is not, as is sometimes believed, ascribable to the nonadaptability of a social and religious tradition that paralyzes every modern development. On the contrary, it is due to the destruction of the ethical and social balance of a system and its replacement with concepts belonging to other civilizations, which have only led to the spreading of disorder under the pretext of a necessary adaptation to new conditions. It seems probable, however, that India will again find prosperity and harmony when external pressures cease to paralyze its development.

APPENDIX 1

THE THIRTY-TWO SCIENCES

The very fact of the four aims of life implies a conception of man, his destiny, and his place in creation that is fundamentally different from that of animal societies. Man is not merely a more developed and perfected animal, and since his very beginning, he has had a special role in the world. The realization of the four aims of life depends on the experience, knowledge, and skills that mankind has acquired history. This body of knowledge has been codified in the form of thirty-two sciences and sixty-four arts, constituting the subjects of traditional Hindu teaching. In the *Niti*, Shukra-acharya explains that "although there is theoretically an indefinite number of arts and sciences, the most important may be classified into categories of which the others can be considered as developments or offshoots."

Shukra-acharya also defines the principle used to distinguish sciences from arts. "Whatever can be explained entirely by means of words is a science, while whatever even a deaf-mute can understand is an art."

The first four sciences concern the study of a body of texts known to the Hindus as *Veda* (Knowledge). The object of the Veda is the set of cosmic laws that fashioned the Universe and preceded its creation. These texts were composed by visionary sages, giving, in a symbolic and hermetic form, a glimpse of those cosmic laws whose knowledge is useful. They are divided into four sections, forming the first four sciences, which are these:

Knowledge of Rhythms or Meters, or *Rig Veda* (1)

Knowledge of Contents, or *Yajur Veda* (2)

Knowledge of Harmonies (astral and sonorous), or *Sama Veda* (3)

Knowledge of Subtle Correspondences, or *Atharva Veda* (4)

The definitions of the Vedas given here, as well as the interpretation of the terms referring to them, are those currently used in traditional Brahman teaching. The Brahmans consider that these texts have been revealed to man and possess a hidden meaning. Modern Indologists see the Vedas from a completely different point of view, as a sort of primitive Aryan folklore, and consequently translate them in quite another fashion that ignores traditional classifications. For the Hindus, these texts are derived from concentrated formulas known as *mantras,* in which each letter and each syllable have multiple symbolic meanings and can be interpreted only with the aid of keys, which vary according to the aspect of the world considered. There are thirty-two keys for each of the Vedic mantras, corresponding to the thirty-two sciences, which can be reduced to the cosmic and fundamental laws that form the essence of the Vedic text. The apparent meaning is of minor importance, serving mostly to hide the true meaning.

Vedic texts fall into two groups: the *Samhitas,* or collections, comprising a body of secret formulas presented as hymns, to which magical powers are attributed; and the *Brahmanas,* or sacerdotal texts, explaining the use of the Samhita formulas in religious or magical rites. The philosophical texts known as "approaches" (Upanishads) are later and more specific additions to the basic Vedic texts.

According to tradition, many Vedic texts have been lost, and those known today under this name are only a small part. Since the transmission of Vedic formulas is considered valid only if it is oral, texts written or learned from a book are dead and lose their magic power.

Four applied sciences derived from the basic Vedic texts are known as secondary Vedas (*Upavedas*) and are the "science of long life," or medicine (*Ayur Veda*) (5), derived from the Knowledge of Rhythms; the "science of weapons," or martial arts (*Dhanur Veda*) (6), derived from the Knowledge of Contents; the "science of celestial bards," or music (*Gandharva Veda*) (7), derived from the Knowledge of Harmonies; and the "science of the secret nature of things," or magic (*Tantra*) (8), derived from the Knowledge of Subtle Correspondences.

Six technical sciences are also directly connected with the Vedas, since they form the basis for ritual language and the determination of propitious times. They are known as *Vedangas* and are annexes to the Vedas. The first is "Teaching" (*Shiksha*) (9), which explains the correct pronunciation of the sacred langua-ge and is vital for the magical effect of the ritual formulas. The second is the "Technique of the Rites" (*Kalpa*) (10), which comprise two kinds, "revealed" (*shrauta*) and "traditional" (*smarta*). Then comes "Philology, Semantics, and Grammar" (*Vyakarana*) (11), explaining the nature and structure of language; the "Symbolic Etymologies" (*Nirukta*) (12), dealing with the secret meaning of words and their ritual usage; the "Poetic Meters" (*Chhanda*) (13), which associates the magical value of rhythm with words; and finally "Astrology" (*Jyotisha*) (14), which determines the propitious moment for every ritual action.

Philosophy is divided into six branches, called "points of view" (*darshana*). The first three are different approaches for trying to understand and interpret the enigma of the perceptible and transcendental Universe. The other three points of view are the methods corresponding to the three approaches. Each point of view starts from a different postulate and uses different ways of reasoning in order to reach its postulated conclusion. The interpretation of the phenomenal world using these various methods leads to

162

different and often contradictory results. By means of these very contradictions, some idea of the real nature of the world, beyond the limited and tendentious image given by our perceptions, can be reached. Thus, according to the darshanas, experimental science (*Vaisheshika*) can only be atheistic. Observation of natural phenomena can never lead to the certitude or even the probability of the existence of a god. A scholar may believe in God on another level, but he cannot allow this notion to enter his reasoning on a scientific level, since otherwise his science would no longer be scientific.

On the other hand, on the cosmological level (*Sankhya*), on which a theoretical world is reconstructed for comparison with the world of appearances, the notion of a prime cause, a personal or impersonal directive will, appears as a necessity. Cosmology, which also includes speculations regarding the nature of atoms and star systems, is therefore somewhat pantheistic. Furthermore, both introspection and the experience of mystics indicate the real presence of a divine being, for which reason Yoga is deistic.

It cannot be said that any of these approaches is truer than any other, since each is realistic in its own field. The notion of multiple and eventually contradictory relative truths, coexisting on different levels and corresponding to the various human means of investigation, whether observation, thought, or intuition, has been a remarkable instrument in the formation of Hindu thought.

The first point of view corresponds to the ritual vision of the world, called *Mimansa*, "reflection" (15), or *Purva-mimansa*, "anterior reflection." We have already seen that the ritual concept of life is a fundamental aspect of Hindu thought. All symbols, such as word, gesture, and form, that serve as a basis for ritual can become means of communication, not only between men but between different worlds and the various orders of creation. The ethic that attributes to our actions a positive value reacting on our individual self and destiny is based on the same concept: the supernatural value of words, actions, and gestures. Mimansa is thus a science of religion, explaining the grounds of the rites and delving into technical possibilities. Moreover, from the Hindu point of view, all actions have a ritual value and should be accomplished as rites: alimentary rites, sleeping rites, sexual rites, rites of giving and receiving, rites of learning, rites of work, and so on.

Mimansa also includes a critical review of the sacred texts used as a basis for ritual. The methods of this scholarly commentary are defined in Jaimini's sutras on Mimansa, on the basis of certain principles such as lack of precedents (*apurva*), choice of eventual alternatives (*niyama*), limitations to what is explicitly expressed (*parishankhya*), and illustrations or examples not to be taken literally (*arthavada*).

Cosmology, or the "Science of Number" (*Sankhya*) (16), is the method corresponding to Mimansa, studying the twenty-five "principles of existence" called *tattvas* (quiddities, or things in themselves). At the origin of all matter, form, sensation and thought, we always find a relation between forces, energies, or tendencies, operating in an immaterial substratum, whose only expression is mathematical. In order to understand the nature of the world, cosmology constructs a theoretical universe in the abstract and compares it with the perceptible or apparent universe to see to what extent the latter's nature can be explained. Ancient Sankhya was one of the most important branches of Hindu philosophical thought, but the very difficulty of its complex data made its widespread teaching almost impossible.

Moreover, most of its texts were left aside and have disappeared, although a certain number still exist and have never been edited but could be recovered. Their study, however, is fraught with considerable difficulties of terminology and would require a very wide knowledge of the mathematical and physical theories of the ancient world. As taught today, Sankhya is a much more restricted system, built on the *Sankhya-sutras* of the sage Kapila, and limiting itself to the twenty-five tattvas. It does not recognize the possibility of a personal god, creator of the Universe, but of two interacting causal entities, known as Person (*Purusha*) and Nature (*Prakriti*).

For Sankhya, the first "principle of existence" is Universal or Cosmic Intelligence (*Mahat Tattva*), while the "notion of individuality" (*ahamkara*) is merely a later manifestation from which flow the spheres of perception and thought.

The point of view most often mentioned by superficial students of Hindu thought is metaphysics, *Vedanta* (17), or "End of Knowledge," which is also known as "Ulterior Reflection" (*Uttara-Mimansa*). In the Vedanta we find the notions of a neuter and impersonal substratum, called the Immensity (*Brahman*) and of a "creative illusion" (*Maya*), which is "oriented energy" (*Shakti*). The nature of this independent, omnipresent and undifferentiated Immensity, without duality, eternal and transcendent, is formed of three inseparable ideas, called Reality, Consciousness, and Joy (*Sat-Cit-Ananda*). It is thus both one and multiple. Indeed, at the root of all existence there must be "something that can be perceived" (*Sat*), a consciousness capable of perceiving (*Chit*), and the perception or the relation of the two, which is sensation (*Ananda*). None of the three can exist without the others. The nature of the creative illusion can only be strictly negative, since it is the contrary of the all, and can therefore be compared to ignorance through which the unreal appears real, like the stretch of rope we believe to be a snake. The limits of our senses, which make us see objects where there are only empty spaces scattered with those energy centers we call atoms, are in effect the work of Maya. The *Vedanta-sutras* of the sage Badarayana are used as a basis for teaching the Vedanta.

Some of the Hindus' most remarkable theories on the relativity of duration, time, space, dimension, matter, and life appear in the Vedanta.

The investigational method corresponding to the data given in the Vedanta is called the Method of Identification (*yoga*) (18), or Method of Reintegration.[1] Yoga envisages knowledge as an inner, direct intuition. Special methods of controlling bodily reflexes and the vital rhythms suspend the agitation of the mind and create

---

1. See Alain Daniélou, *Yoga: Mastering the Secrets of Matter and the Universe* (Rochester, Vt.: Inner Traditions International, 1991).

an inner silence that allows the yogi or adept to direct his will to explore unknown regions of consciousness and utilize latent faculties for the purpose of extra-sensory perception. Hindus consider yoga the most efficacious instrument for investigating the nature of the apparent and transcendent worlds, and a method for realizing the presence and nature of the divine being in itself and in its creation. The experience of mystics is always an experience of yoga, which can be either systematic or simply intuitive and accidental.

Special yoga techniques can produce magic powers, or *Siddhis,* whose realization must, however, be considered an obstacle to the ultimate aim of yoga, which is the liberation of the living being from the world of appearances and reintegration of the individual with the absolute being.

The point of view that appears most familiar is experimental science, or "Study of the Particular" (*Vaisheshika*) (19). What the West calls science belongs to Vaisheshika, in which the sensory organs are used as instruments of knowledge and research, starting from observational data, in order to know and define the nature of the world and the laws that govern it. As already mentioned, Vaisheshika, or science, is necessarily atheistic, since observing the world through the senses gives a biased view. The appearance of things only expresses the limits of our sensory perception; the purpose of appearance is to hide from us the inner nature of things, which cannot be reached by such instruments.

The last point of view, logic (*Nyaya*) (20), is the method corresponding to Vaisheshika, science. It employs the symbols and logical arrangement of language in reasoning as an instrument for reaching conclusions. Logic and its technique, dialectics, are essential instruments for all effective discursive thought and the vital method of all science. With the aid of deduction and various other means of proof, logic deals with six "fundamental aspects of existence" (*tattvas*), which are substance, quality, action, general characteristics, special characteristics, and correlation. Nonexistence (*abhava*) may be considered a seventh aspect.

The proofs (*pramanas*) accepted by logic are—according to Gautama, one of its principal exponents—perception (*pratyak-sha*), deduction (*anumana*), comparison (*upamana*), and dialectics (*shabda*). Kanada, however, recognizes only perception and deduction, considering that they imply all the others.

The factors constituting substance (*dravya*) are of nine kinds and include the elements or spheres of perception of the five senses, to which are added the substrata of duration, space, being, and intelligence. The five elements as envisaged by Hindu philosophy are merely the spheres of perception of the senses. Earth is the sphere of perception of smell; water the sphere of perception of taste; fire the sphere of perception of sight; air the sphere of perception of touch; and ether the sphere of perception of hearing. Sound can only be heard; air is perceived through hearing and touch; fire can be seen, heard, and touched; water is perceptible to all the senses except smell; whereas earth can be perceived by all the senses. The sphere of sound is thus the most abstract of the senses, and nearest to the causal state.

Quality (*guna*) involves twenty-four aspects, which apart from the sensory data (visibility, taste, smell, touch, audibility) include number, independence, hierarchy, succession, form, name, intelligibility, pleasure, sorrow, desire, repulsion, effort, conformity to cosmic law, and divergence from cosmic law.

Action is of five kinds: ascending, descending, contracting, expanding, and translating.

General characteristics are of two orders, according to whether they can be perceived or felt.

Nonexistence is of four kinds: nonexistence in the past, nonexistence by anihilation; nonexistence of one thing in another; absolute nonexistence for all time.

The twenty-first science is History, *Itihasa* (21), "that which happened." History is conceived in the form of stories telling the lives and adventures of ancient kings and revealing various aspects of civilization and culture in a far-removed, idealized past. These epics are usually envisaged as a philosophy of history, seeking to discern the laws of its development, its logic and teaching, in order to draw ethical and political conclusions to serve as an example for mankind. A simple recital of facts proving nothing and interesting no one in particular has always appeared purposeless to the Hindu historian.

The main epics are the *Ramayana* and the *Mahabharata*. The *Ramayana* recounts the adventures of the hero Rama and takes place in what can be considered prehistoric times, since it refers to forests and primitive tribes occupying sites where important towns already flourished as early as the third millennium B.C.E. Several versions of this epic exist, and it must certainly have formed part of the pre-Aryan oral tradition for a very long time. From the literary standpoint, the most important version is Valmiki's, composed in beautiful Sanskrit verse in an unknown period. Other versions exist in several of the Puranas, which largely reflect the broad outlines of the original legend.

The *Mahabharata* is an enormous work combining a large number of traditional information referring to a fratricidal war, which according to Hindu chronology took place in the third millennium B.C.E. It is in fact a symbolic account of the great struggles between the Aryan Kurus from the north and the Dravidian Pandavas for the possession of the cities of the Indus valley.

The *Mahabharata* is a mine of information about the science, customs, religion, and arts of India at various stages of its history. Additions from very different sources have been made to the original, turning it into a vast anthology of human knowledge.

Apart from the legendary accounts of the epics, the first truly historical Hindu chronicles, recounting the military, political, or dynastic events of particular kingdoms, commence only toward the Gupta period, during the sixth century C.E. Important historical documents are found, however, among the Buddhists and Jains, the earliest of which date from the fifth century B.C.E.

The Ancient Chronicles, or Puranas (22) (the word *Purana* simply meaning "ancient") are vast collections of all the ancient knowledge of India since prehistoric times. They include mythological epics, the genealogies of kings, and the legends of heros, and they summarize the geographical, historical, and scientific knowledge of very ancient times. The Itihasa epics are also included in abridged form but are placed in the general picture of Indian civilization and history.

The Puranas are mostly transcriptions of very ancient traditions that had been transmitted orally for centuries in now forgotten languages. In their present form, they were compiled or translated into Sanskrit during a relatively recent period, but references more ancient than the texts themselves, by Greek historians and Buddhist and Jain chroniclers, show that their contents were well known long before their current versions were compiled. The most ancient genealogies in the Puranas go back as far as the sixth millennium B.C.E. and are of enormous interest for the history of mankind. As with all traditions that have been transmitted orally for a long time, it is often difficult to sort out the most ancient elements from the agglomerations of the centuries. Several of the Puranas, at least in part, antedate the Aryan invasions, and thus the Vedas and even the Indus civilization. The pre-Aryan religion of India, Shaivism, was for centuries rejected by the Aryans as diabolical. Only when Shaivism was reintegrated with Hinduism were the Puranas rehabilitated and translated into Sanskrit. Even more ancient versions exist in Dravidian languages.

There are thirty-six Puranas, of which eighteen are considered to be principal and eighteen secondary. Certain of them only exist today in fragmentary form, whereas others are still extremely important, such as the *Skanda Purana,* with its twenty-two volumes. The body of the eighteen principal Puranas still includes nearly one million Sanskrit verses. The secondary Puranas have only been partly edited, and many of their texts have probably been lost. Taken together, their quantity should be about the same as that of the principal Puranas. It would certainly be possible to recover many of them from the numerous manuscript libraries of India, some of which have never been explored or catalogued.

The twenty-third science is formed by the *Smritis,* or traditions (23). These texts are very numerous and include secular codes of ethics and laws. The best known are the Law of Manu (*Manu smriti*), the Laws of Yajñavalkya (*Yajñavalkya smriti*) and the *Niti* (politics) of Shukra. There are hundreds of other Smritis, representing the whole legal system of traditional India and still used as the basis of Hindu law. They contain all the rules of life for the various castes and different ages of life.

In India, the various heterodox systems of philosophy, grouped around materialistic and atheistic currents of thought, are classified together as "Negative Opinions" (*Nastika mata*) (24). Atheistic thought naturally rejects the possibility of revelation and thus attributes no particular value to the Vedas and other sacred books. It denies the existence of a personal god and accepts only the evidence of the senses as a means of proof. Consciousness and thought are considered to be fermentations of matter, and death is the total dissolution of the human being. Pleasure is the only aim of life. The first theoretician of materialistic philosophy was the sage Brihaspati, but the most famous and most violent of its apostles was Charvaka, whose name is now synonymous with atheism.

The *Artha Shastra* (25), referred to above, unites economic and political theories with the aim of developing the prosperity and organization of the State.

The *Kama Shastra* (26) describes erotic science in all its technical and psychological aspects.

The *Shilpa Shastra* (27), or "Art of Construction," is the science of architecture, including all the plastic arts, sculpture, and painting. Temples, palaces, and houses are all built according to symbolic diagrams, or *Yantras*. The direction of space, the location of openings, and the orientation of the rooms according to their destination play an important role in the equilibrium of the people therein. There are many treatises of *Shilpa Shastra*, often illustrated with sketches and drawings to explain in precise detail the various construction techniques, calculations, and styles of architecture for temples and palaces; the proportions and rules of sculpture; the preparation of colors; and fresco techniques and composition.[2]

There follows Poetic Art (*Kavya*) (28), which explains the various meters, their use in poetry, figures of speech, the ornaments and composition of language, images, and the nine emotions (*rasas*) and the art of expressing them.

---

2. See Alice Boner, *New Light on the Sun Temple Konarka*, Benares, 1974.

The study of living languages (*Desha bhasha*) (29) and dialects (*Daishiki*) constitutes the twenty-ninth science. In the often obscure texts relating to this science, phrases are often encountered that were borrowed from long-vanished languages. Their transcription into the phonetic Sanskrit alphabet can sometimes give a fairly clear picture of what they were like.

"Words of Occasion" (*Avasarokti*) (30) include proverbs, sayings, definitions, and replies, particularly pertaining to philosophical questions.

"Ionian Philosophy" (*Yavana Mata*) (31) covers not only the philosophy of ancient Greece but all other foreign philosophical concepts, in particular those from the various civilizations of the ancient Western world. Christian and Islamic philosophies were also incorporated later.

The last of the sciences is the "Science of Religions" (*Deshadi dharma*) (32), which is a study of all local or indigenous religions, as well as the forms taken by religious concepts, rites, and beliefs in different parts of the world. For Hindus, the highest principle of government in conquered countries was the absolute respect of their religion, rites, customs, and laws. By virtue of this principle, persecuted religions have always found refuge and protection in India.

APPENDIX 2
THE SIXTY-FOUR ARTS

Although techniques and arts are theoretically innumerable, Sanskrit treatises consider that they can be reduced to the symbolic number of sixty-four, to which sixty-four minor arts are sometimes added. According to the *Shukra Niti,* these arts are divided into two categories: the arts of pleasure and the magical arts. Among the arts of pleasure, including the minor arts, are numbered twenty-four arts of action, twenty of games, sixteen erotic arts, and four noble arts. There are also sixty-four magical arts, which include the minor arts.

The lists of the arts differ according to the various texts, the principal arts remaining the same and others being added to reach the traditional number of sixty-four. If all the lists were combined, the result would be more than two hundred. This chapter will therefore be limited to the ones that seem to be distinct forms of art, since the art of making flower crowns is not really distinct from the art of making flower earrings or necklaces, and the art of the expert in precious stones does not greatly differ from the cutter's. The number of arts is therefore not as important as the picture of civilization they supply. Certain arts are applied sciences; others are handicrafts. The principal arts listed here follow the definitions given by the *Vishnu-dharmottara purana,* as well as by Shukra's *Niti* and the Jayamangala commentary on the *Kama Sutra.* Shukra's list is probably more ancient than the Jayamangala's and antedates the Christian era by several centuries.

The first of the arts is song, born together with, and possibly even before, language, and inseparable from it. Its technique continues and develops in musical instruments, whose utilization constitutes the second art. From music, dance (3) is born. (According to Shukra, dance is the first of the arts, in which gesture is the basic aspect, speech being but a limited aspect of language.) Dance is divided into two main branches: harmonious movement and expressive gesture. The various kinds of dance thus accord with the various combinations of mime, rhythm, and plastic movement. For Shukra, the various elements of the dance are mimed action, pure technique, plasticity, sentiment, grace, and the evocation of the nine emotional states of man, which include love, vanity, laughter, anger, sorrow, disgust, pity, astonishment, and peace. Dance is a basic art, found among all peoples in all forms of civilization.

Painting (4), the first of the static arts, fixes the motions of dance and the expression of faces. Shukra defines the art of painting according to six criteria: technique, proportion, the fusion of beauty and expression, likeness, harmony of colors, and composition. The art of fresco painting has played a major role in India. The walls of palaces and private houses were formerly covered with frescos, both inside and out. In the palaces, covered galleries were known as picture galleries. Among the most ancient surviving frescos are those found on the walls of the chambers and assembly halls of monasteries carved out of the rock, of which the ones at Ajanta, starting from 300 B.C.E., are the most famous.

Among the secondary arts connected with painting are calligraphy (5), wood-carving for printing purposes (6), and designs traced on the floor (7) with flowers and colored grains of rice. Even now, the entrance and floors of the houses are still decorated during festivals with these ephemeral and marvel-lous carpets. Mosaics (8) are the concrete version of the same decorations.

Sculpture (9) is a hybrid art, since it is connected with architecture, which is a science, and with painting, which it resembles in relief. Sculpture is very important in the building of temples and in rites, since when the sculptor observes the correct proportions of the various parts of the body and inscribes them within a magic diagram, the work attracts the real presence of the divinities represented.

Similarly related to architecture are furniture (10) and furnishing techniques, the art of bed arrangement, carpentry (11), and interior decoration (12).

Certain arts are associated with language and with the theater, including first of all diction (13) and oratory (14), then reading aloud, especially choral recitation (15), memorizing (16), extemporizing poetry (17), the use of poetic meters and word rhythms (18), and the composition of dictionaries (19). These are followed by arts connected with the theater, such as mime proper (20), which differs from danced mime, riddles (21), ma-rionettes (22), and the arts of costume (23) and makeup (24).

The art of dressing and adornment play an important role in urban communities. The bases of the art of dressing are spinning (25), weaving (26), and stitching and embroidery (27). These are followed by the tailor's art, cutting (28), and dyeing (29), which includes the coloring of teeth, skin, and cloth. The main ornaments comprise flower necklaces and adornments for the hair and ears (30), and jewelry—necklaces, earrings, girdles, and hair ornaments of gold and precious stones (31). The making of perfumes (32) is also an important art, followed by the art of the hairdresser and barber (33), massage and surgery (34), and finally, erotic art (35).

Among the arts pertaining to food, the main ones are culinary art (36), and the preparation of sweet, alcoholic, or intoxicating drinks (37), dairy products (38), milk drinks and cheeses, herbs (39), and aphrodisiacs (40).

Among handcrafts, the first is the making of stringed instruments (41). Treatises on music give detailed descriptions of musical instruments and the art of making them. Instruments are divided into four categories: strings, wind, drums, and percussion (gongs, bells, cymbals, xylophones). These are followed by such minor arts as basket-making (42), glass-making (43), ceramics (44), the construction of leather articles and footgear (45), laundering (46), and domestic arts (47).

The agricultural arts are essential to society and include irrigation (48) and the construction of canals and aqueducts, then agriculture (49), horticulture (50), and arboriculture (51).

The industrial techniques include mining (52), metallurgy and alloys (53), cutting precious stones (54), and minting coins (55). These are followed by mechanics (56) and the arts of building machines, especially steam devices "using fire, water, and steam to make machines move" (*Shukra Niti*), fountains (57), hydraulic organs (58), war machines for launching projectiles (59), and chariots, boats, and other means of transport (60). Then come strategy (61) and the training of horses and driving of chariots (62). One of the most delicate techniques referred to is the construction of precision instruments, especially for measuring time and distance and for calculating the movement of the stars (63).

Among sports (64), those usually mentioned include physical culture, team games, wrestling, boxing, and swimming.

Games fill an important place among the arts, The first are games of chance, such as dice; they are followed by games of calculation, like checkers, dominos, and cards. Indian cards are round and quite unlike those used in Europe. Among games are also counted the art of arranging cock- or quail-fights, and of training frogs and "talking birds" such as parrots and myna birds. After these come sleight-of-hand, juggling, magic, the interpretation of omens, hypnotism, and metamorphosis. The art of making children play is both difficult and important. Secret languages for private communication, without being understood, coded writing, and messages are also listed as arts.

All these arts, says Shukra-acharya, are the fruits of two main qualities: skill and patience, which are the source of all art.

SOURCES

In writing this book, apart from the oral teachings on which it is based, I have utilized the following works: The *Purushartha visheshanka,* a special edition of the Hindi review *Siddhanta* on the four aims of life (Benares, 1956); the *Dharma Dipika,* a selection of Sanskrit texts on the four aims of life (Benares, 1942); the various Smritis, including the *Manu* smriti and the *Yajñavalkya* smriti; the various Puranas; the *Mahabharata*; the *Shukra Niti* by Shukra-acharya; the *Artha Shastra* by Kautilya; the *Kama Sutra* by Vatsyayana and its commentaries; as well as numerous other texts, quotations from which occasionally appear.

INDEX